CREATING KIND AND compassionate KIDS

CREATING KIND AND compassionate KIDS

Classroom Activities to Enhance Self-Awareness, Empathy, and Personal Growth in Grades 3-6

Deborah S. Delisle and James R. Delisle, Ph.D.

PRUFROCK PRESS INC.
WACO, TEXAS

Prufrock Press Inc.
P.O. Box 8813
Waco, TX 76714-8813
Phone: (800) 998-2208
Fax: (800) 240-0333
http://www.prufrock.com

Dedication

This book is dedicated to the thousands of students with whom we have worked. They have taught us about compassion and caring and have permitted us to help them become leaders. To each of them, we say "thanks" for helping us to grow a part of our hearts. Most importantly, we also dedicate this book to our favorite "grandbuddy," Wyatt. Like his parents, Wyatt warms our hearts every day simply by being who he is. We hope his life is filled with great joy and wonderous adventures. His presence in our lives is our greatest present.

TABLE OF CONTENTS

Introduction

The difference between a goal and a dream is attitude. To the logical mind, a goal seems realistic; the term itself implies a predetermined point at which you know you've succeeded. A dream, on the other hand, relies on hunch and hope rather than logic; it is airier, but less bulky, than a goal. Its fulfillment depends more on vision and imagination than on planned, structured steps. More loosely defined than a goal, a dream tends to meander down uncharted paths. In fact, when a dream is reached, it may be a surprise even to the person who conceived it.

Goals and Dreams for Students

In our early years as educators, the authors of this book often considered dreams and goals to be the same. Out of fear that we might not succeed, we did not always directly pursue our teaching goals, and we tried to make our subjective dream of being effective teachers too realistic. We thought, for example, that all of our classroom lessons had to be as exciting and memorable as a Disney movie; when they weren't, we often disappointed ourselves. By mistaking our goals for student learning with our dreams for effective teaching, we sidestepped many important lessons that could have benefited our students. These might not have been perfect lessons, but they would have been meaningful nonetheless.

When we encounter past students who have become teachers or parents of students with whom we now interact, these exchanges remind us of the impact of distinguishing our aims (goals) from our missions (dreams). Based on reflections and feedback from these parents and newly minted teachers, we recognize the sustainability of lessons that impact the mind as well as the heart. Social-emotional skills—like a sense of perspective on success or failure—take time to develop. When former students share what they remember most about being in our classrooms, they recall their feelings about certain lessons rather than specific content. Even as parents, our hearts sing when our son recalls a teacher who believed in him more than he believed in himself. Effective teachers do that—by choice and by making lessons come alive. The old bromide is true: "Kids don't care how much you know until they know how much you care."

To teach a child to read may be our aim, but to help a child appreciate the beauty of written words is our mission. Getting to know their community is a laudable goal for our students, but envisioning the possible ways they can serve that community is a lifelong dream we seek for them. Using higher level thinking skills will expand children's minds; developing empathy and concern for others will develop their emotional intelligence.

Our collective years in education have taught us a very important lesson: The most relevant and lasting learning experiences involve emotional skills. We'd like to think that classrooms everywhere would operate on the principle of designing "lessons of life." Teachers often speak about teaching the "whole child," but merely stating the goal without living the principle can be hollow. After all, long after students have mastered multiplication tables and memorized the capitals of the world, they will assume their roles as citizens. The most able mathematician, adroit political leader, articulate teacher, skilled surgeon, or savvy business owner contributes more to society when applying technical and professional know-how from a foundation of self-confidence, compassion, respect for others, and stewardship.

Educators have both the opportunity and the obligation to prepare students fully to assume their roles as global citizens. How? By helping them to acquire academic skills and knowledge, certainly. Yet, equally important is helping them appreciate themselves and care about others—and providing concrete ways for them to act upon their caring. Thus, we present *Creating Kind and Compassionate Kids*. Within these pages are examples of lessons we have designed and taught to help us reach our dream, our mission: allowing all students to experience the joy of learning about themselves while acting in the service of others.

About the Activities

In designing these lessons, we paid attention to many solid principles of learning espoused by respected educators. All of the activities contain the following elements.

They involve both cognitive and social-emotional learning. The activities call on students to think, feel, and react simultaneously. Based mostly in the content areas of language arts and social studies, these activities also contain aspects of innovation, introspection, or humor—elements that help to make content memorable. For example, Activity 1: Grate Misteaks provides the cognitive lesson that mistakes sometimes lead to important inventions; it also invites students to explore the affective concept that no one is perfect. In Activity 10: Filling Our Own Shoes, students learn about individuals who displayed strength and character in their lives and then reflect on friends and family who help them build their own character. All of the lessons in this book address several social and emotional attributes.

They are experiential. Each activity is based upon respect for students and the belief that students already know much about life and are curious to learn more. Too often, it is assumed that adults do the teaching while kids do the learning. These activities blur this teaching-learning division by making learning an active, cooperative endeavor. You know your students best; thus, we encourage you to rely on your knowledge to adapt the lessons to best meet your students' cognitive and social-emotional developments.

They are open-ended. All activities in our book can be interpreted and completed according to the individual ideas of the teacher and students. Students should not be reluctant to complete the work out of fear that the final product might be "wrong" or unacceptable. In fact, students will express themselves more creatively and benefit more fully when teachers allow them to complete the activities without regard to a grade. Each lesson has a clearly defined beginning, middle, and end, as well as a tangible product showing the results of students' explorations. In some cases, the product might be a piece of introspective writing; in others, it might be a community service project to help their global neighbors. Your students' conversations may suggest possibilities for additional products. "How can we share our learning?" is a question of great value for every activity.

They are teacher- and student-tested. We are not asking you to teach a lesson that we ourselves have not taught. Every activity has withstood the toughest test of all: a hands-on trial with students in heterogeneously grouped elementary and middle school classroom settings. The samples of student work accompanying many lessons are just a handful of the numerous original, wise, and multifaceted responses the activities have elicited from our students. The samples are intended as models and, as such, are excellent springboards for your students' creative endeavors. Share these examples with students or use them for your own personal reference. We have seldom found that students will want to produce something that looks very much like the student samples; rather, they see them as exemplars that encourage them to stretch their minds.

They can be personalized to suit teachers' and students' needs. Although the activities are broadly designed for heterogeneously grouped classrooms of students in grades 3–6, teachers at the primary or middle school levels should be able to adjust many of the activities with little trouble. In fact, we have used them as springboards for learning in both grades 7 and 8, adapting the lessons to meet the developmental stages of these students. Consider deepening the activities both in content and expectation to personalize lessons for more mature groups of students.

Likewise, we recognize that every classroom has its own unique personality. We encourage you to mold and reshape the activities in consideration of and respect for your students' needs, strengths, interests, and weaknesses (yes, even those). Remember, no single book—including this one—is appropriate for all students of any age. Select the activities you wish to use, as you know your students' preferences, likes, and dislikes. Flexible in both scope and time, each activity has been designed so you can adapt it to your students' needs—personalized learning, for sure! You'll find that some activities will work best within individual classrooms. Others will be equally effective in a team setting of multiple classrooms. Still others are appropriate for schoolwide participation. Some lessons are intended for one class session, while others may extend for longer periods of time. In each instance, we will include the most effective time frame we have found for conducting the lessons, although you are encouraged to adapt this to your own situation. Read through the activity and determine what goals are important for your students; then match them within a workable time frame to fit your schedule as well as your instructional style.

They can be holistically evaluated. With increased attention given to student evaluation, there is the inevitable question, "How do I grade these projects?" From our perspective, the purpose of the activities, as designed and field-tested, is to enhance self-awareness, expand leadership opportunities, and generate creativity and compassion. As such, the activities are not intended to be evaluated with an arbitrary letter or number grade. Doing so will give students too little direction in how to improve their work and may stifle their blossoming sense of self and awareness of others. Instead, we encourage holistic evaluation.

Holistic Evaluation

What It Is

Reviewing the writing as a whole and providing comments that:
- offer another chance to improve,
- propose specific ideas as to how to deepen one's thinking,
- share constructive ideas for growth and improvement, and
- ask the student, "What did you learn?" (*Note.* From time to time, ask students, "What did you learn about yourself as a result of participating in this activity?")

What It Isn't

Letter/number grades that:
- say, "One strike, you're out!";
- dissect individual segments;
- provide little, if any, constructive feedback on strengths and weaknesses;
- suggest there is only one acceptable response; and
- ask the student, "What did you earn?"

How to Use the Activities

Each activity begins with a brief introduction followed by information about learning objectives, materials, time frame, and, if necessary, preparation guidelines. A few activities provide useful background information as well. Activity steps are clearly numbered. Many activities include "For Surefire Success" hints for making the activity fully effective. You will also find suggestions for adapting or expanding many activities for use with your own class, other classes, families, and the community.

With some activities, we suggest related books and other resources that may be of interest to you or your students. You will find descriptions and publishing information about these optional materials in the Recommended Resources section.

Although most of the activities include a writing component, feel free to substitute other means of communication (e.g., audio, video, drawing, skits) if you'd rather not assign a writing activity or if some of your students have difficulty writing. Additionally, these alternate forms may meet requirements for a specific grade-level standard.

The sequence for using the activities is entirely up to you. Start by choosing those that spark your interest or that seem particularly fitting for your group of students. A few activities will work especially well at the beginning of the school year. You will also find these activities helpful when there have been changes in the makeup of your classroom or when people need to get reacquainted after extended holiday or term breaks.

Time frames reflect our experience using the activities. These will vary depending on the size of your class or group, the ages of your students, the time of day, length of your class time, and your own teaching style. You may find it helpful to plan your own time frame for each activity step.

Let's Begin!

Teachers, students, families—we're all in this thing called "education" together. By combining our talents, we can surely broaden our students' minds and, in doing so, fulfill some of our own goals and dreams. After all, what better beginning to life can we give our students than the gift of learning to grow their own emotional intelligence? We hope this book becomes a valued resource in achieving this important goal. As we always say, *onward*!

Creating an Invitational Classroom and School

Remember the classroom rules that met you on your first day of school each year? Sometimes the rules were short and to the point. At other times they went on for pages, compiled by teachers who apparently never considered the idea that "less is more." Whether the rules were brief or seemingly endless, they probably used words like *don't*, *no*, and *never*:

- Don't talk out of turn.
- No food in class.
- Never run in the halls.

There was very little encouragement to do anything positive; rather, you were surrounded by warnings of what not to do. Sometimes, you might have even wondered, "If I can't do that, what can I do?" Unfortunately, this remains true for many students today. Consider a day as uninviting as this:

Sandy waits in a cold rain for a school bus that is already 20 minutes late. As the bus pulls up, water sprays her new jeans. Climbing onto the bus, she's greeted with the driver's gruff, "C'mon—I'm not your private chauffeur, you know. Hurry up!" As Sandy takes her seat, the kids sitting two rows back start taunting her by calling her "Wet Pants." She tries to ignore them, but it's not easy.

The first person she meets upon arrival at school is the custodian, who warns the students not to drip on the just-waxed floor. Sandy scurries by to avoid detection. Once at her desk, she looks up at the board and reads, "Homework that is not turned in by the opening bell earns a grade of zero." Sandy's stomach sinks as she is unable to find in her backpack the three pages of homework she worked on for 2 hours.

The school day begins. Misbehaving students get their names written on the board, with a check mark for each additional offense. Sandy sees that one more check mark next to Brian's name will mean no recess for the entire class! The class makes it to recess somehow. As students choose teams for kickball, it's clear that no one wants Sandy. As usual, she's chosen last, and her teammates groan as she joins them. Then, for no reason at all, one student from her team punches another one, forcing a schoolyard monitor to intervene. "When you go inside," says the monitor, "you will each write 'I will not fight at recess' 10 times. I expect to see your sentences before recess tomorrow."

With the day almost over, Sandy can't wait to go home. Just before dismissal, her teacher announces the results of last Friday's math test. When she hears "Sandy—C, 72%," Sandy grabs her paper, embarrassed, and ducks back into her seat.

The bus ride home is quiet. Hardly anyone is in the mood for talking.

For Sandy, school is a series of uninviting hurdles, a minefield of potential embarrassments waiting to explode. In an environment so mired in negativity, what is there to sustain students' long-term interest? Although Sandy's scenario seems extreme, it is still experienced by some of our most needy students. The negative impact of a day even half as bad as Sandy's will eventually take its toll on most students.

Invite Learning With a Positive and Supportive Climate

Consider how teachers might invite students like Sandy to engage and succeed in school. Imagine a classroom with rules like these:

- Walking in the halls prevents accidents.
- Be mature and serious during fire drills.
- When in groups, talk in 6-inch voices.
- Ask before you use.
- People can be hurt by words and actions, so use both carefully.
- Please remember: Kindness is contagious!
- Everyone needs a friend.

Focusing on what students already do right and on what they can do fosters a productive and dynamic classroom and school. Students recognize what the school staff values. Educators need to assume that students want to learn and be respected, no matter how they look or act or where they live. When students are given reasonable amounts of challenge and freedom, they will behave appropriately in classrooms. If educators communicate these positive expectations, many worries about classroom management will evaporate as incidents of misbehavior diminish. Further, teachers will do more than set an expectation for cooperation; they will invite students to take part in a truly cooperative learning experience.

Two of the strongest advocates of invitational education are William Purkey and John Novak. In *Inviting School Success: A Self-Concept Approach to Teaching, Learning, and Democratic Practice*, they reviewed the links between students' attitudes toward school and their school success. Purkey and Novak (1996) stressed four principles for invitational education:

- People are able, valuable, and responsible, and should be treated accordingly.
- Teaching should be a cooperative activity.
- People possess relatively untapped potential in all areas of human development.
- This potential can best be realized by places, policies, and programs that are specifically designed to invite development and by people who are personally and professionally inviting to themselves and others.

Inviting School Success seems even more relevant in an era when the social and emotional aspects of children's lives often take a backseat to their academic performance. When students are invited to become partners in their own and their peers' learning, they recognize that educators anticipate success and cooperation rather than negative behaviors. There are many ways schools can implement invitational education, and the "inviters" involve all stakeholders, beyond the teachers whose jobs involve direct and sustained daily contact with students. As the example of Sandy suggests, all people in any school community—including the principal, office personnel, and support staff—play important roles in making a school the kind of place where learning and belonging go hand in hand.

Foster Positive Learning Environments Schoolwide

Some principles of invitational education involve behavioral expectations and classroom environments, while others are focused on curriculum content and instructional practices. For example, a school with a policy against all forms of academic acceleration dismisses the talents of a second grader whose math skills are at a fifth-grade competency. On the other hand, a school where learning is individualized to the point that children flow freely from teacher to teacher, depending on their unique levels of ability, allows students to tap into their talents without regard to grade-level placement. Is it more difficult to operate a school based on the latter approach? Of course, but educators are responsible for doing the job necessary to fully promote student achievement and to ensure students gain a respect for their talents and those of others. In establishing a positive and respectful school culture, you must examine school and district policies and practices that may inhibit learning or positive behaviors. Together with your colleagues, arrive at alternative methods of promoting achievement and positive student behaviors by implementing ideas that anticipate the positive over the negative.

Invite Effort by Involving and Motivating Students

Praising students for good behavior and performance is a common practice of classroom management that seems in concert with the goals of invitational education. Giving too much praise or too many rewards, however, teaches students to work for the wrong reasons. In "Are We Spoiling Our Kids With Too Much Praise?", Pocock (2017) cited studies showing that the more praise children receive, the less likely they are to be intrinsically interested in continuing to pursue the endeavor. Using examples that are all too familiar—like giving every entrant into a sports match or spelling bee an award or praising a child for getting 100% on a math test that required no mental strain at all—Pocock indicated that teachers may be fueling a generation of narcissists. Giving feedback to children that focuses on either their efforts or highlights a specific aspect of their work is fine, but the mere doling out of praise for every task they complete has unintended consequences, including a decline in their interest in completing the praised activity again. Additionally, telling kids they are special because they can do tasks expected at their age level gives a false sense of what can be accomplished and what higher goals can actually be reached. Once, when walking through a first-grade hallway, we observed a bulletin board titled "We are special because . . ." with various students' names linked to a comment about why each was special. Kids and their families could immediately observe the distinction between John who is special because he can "print his name" to Sophia who can "count to 100." Such a public "declaration" of different student strengths may actually subvert the intended goal of recognizing students' accomplishments.

The same principle applies when teachers offer praise for nonacademic pursuits. So, when sixth grader Dwayne gets praised in front of his classmates for opening his textbook to the appropriate page ("Thank you, Dwayne. I really like how you went to that page so quickly."), the teacher might actually be undercutting the likelihood that the behavior will occur again. Why? Because Dwayne was just doing as he was told, and now he may be harassed by classmates who perceive that Dwayne made them look bad.

Another aspect of praise that must be reconsidered is how frequently it is given en masse. For example, when teachers praise good grades orally ("There were five As in math today—I'm so proud of you!"), they seldom consider that for some of those "A" students, the task was, indeed, difficult and their accomplishment noteworthy; however, other students may have put in little or no effort to earn that A, as the task may have been easy for them. It doesn't take long for most students to recognize the emptiness of this kind of praise. Alternatively, what does this praise for A grades do for students who may have gotten a lower grade, yet showed vast improvement over their previous attempts? Their work and their efforts are virtually ignored. The best and truest rewards of all are the feelings of joy and accomplishment that accompany a fulfilling learning experience, which may have little to do with a specific grade that was received.

Feedback that focuses on these benefits of learning will stay with a child long after shallow comments like "Great job!" have been forgotten. Personalized comments strengthen behaviors of kids—and this is equally as important for academically successful students as for those who struggle. For example, when talented writers receive an A without specific comments, they may not know what is particularly strong about their writing. By providing comments such as "Your vocabulary continues to be strong," or "Your use of complex sentences is improving," students are informed with specific details about what earned them a high grade and are more apt to focus on these in future writing. On the other hand, those students who find writing to be a challenge already know they may never receive an A. Thus, positive encouragement in the form of comments such as "Your writing is showing an increased understanding of how complete sentences are formed," or "Your use of descriptive vocabulary in the three highlighted sentences makes me want to read more," provides specific details on which student may rely in future endeavors.

The activities in *Creating Kind and Compassionate Kids* are designed to allow students to express themselves in ways that interest them intrinsically. You'll find that there are virtually no right or wrong answers to these activities; rather, each one is open-ended enough that kids who struggle with writing may find just as much success as those who excel.

Invite Risk-Taking by Allowing Mistakes

Quick! Name one thing that every person has in common but likes to keep hidden from everyone else. Give up? Take a guess. It's okay if you guess wrong and make a mistake; in fact, mistakes are the point. The common thread that weaves through people's collective lives is human frailty: the propensity to make mistakes again and again. Of course, most people don't like to admit to being less than perfect, factory seconds in a world of designer originals. However, truth be known, everyone is just a little bit off base, at least some of the time.

Think about it: Star athletes successfully complete just a fraction of their passes or stolen bases. Television and movie actors audition for dozens of parts before getting a role. Renowned scientists take years to perfect one formula or theorem, ever conscious that each "error" provides one more example of how something doesn't work. If it's acceptable for the highest paid and most esteemed citizens to make mistakes like these, shouldn't it be acceptable for the kids in our classrooms, too?

Some of the activities in this book allow you to emphasize the idea that mistakes are actually a good thing. Here are some other ways to show your students that mistakes are a necessary and acceptable part of learning.

Display imperfect work. On your walls and bulletin boards, post student work that, although good, is not perfect. Posting only perfection sends the wrong message: that nothing less is acceptable. You may wish to ask students themselves to select and post work they are especially proud of, even if it is a tad imperfect.

Admit your own mistakes. Share with your students your own instances of mistake making. Revisit the memory of going the wrong way down a one-way street. Recount the time you held your spouse's hand at the zoo only to discover that it was somebody (or something) else's hand you were clasping. Share the time when you added salt instead of sugar in your favorite cookie recipe. These situations humanize you in ways that students don't forget. Consider making a school or classroom display in which everyone is encouraged to post (anonymously) situations in which they exclaimed, "Oops!"

Make intentional mistakes. Put an intentional error on a test or homework assignment, awarding an extra point to students who find and correct it. (Be prepared to have them find mistakes you hadn't planned, too!) It may seem like a small thing to extol the virtues of making errors. However, to students who are especially conscious of their own academic, social, and physical imperfections, your willingness to go public with something that most teachers keep to themselves will send a strong message of support. So, go ahead and break a leg (figuratively speaking, of course).

The ABCs of Effective Learning Environments

Actively involve your students in planning their learning activities and outcomes.

Become an advocate for inquiry-based education, in which students discover new facets of themselves and their world.

Concentrate on small steps and successes, as competency seldom arrives in one fluid and sequential process.

Decide to make at least one major change in your teaching style each year, freeing yourself from "I've always done it this way" practices.

Enjoy the lessons as much as your students do—enthusiasm is contagious.

Facilitate meaningful discussions among your students.

Gather engaging resources (e.g., books, videos, websites, TED Talks) for use in planning and carrying out units of study.

Help all students discover and tap into their own talents and interests.

Introduce at least one new unit of study per school year.

Just relax and enjoy your students as they are, not for what you'd like them to become.

Know that you are more important in your students' lives than you may think you are.

Love teaching, and tell your students they make your job feel like not a job at all.

Make time for every student. Notice a new haircut, comment on an unexpected smile, thank a kid for being kind to someone else, or ask why a student seems sad one day.

Negotiate classroom rules with your students.

Often reflect on your educational philosophies, noting if your beliefs match your actions.

Pause periodically to let your students "breathe" by diverting from the curriculum to simply have fun with learning activities.

Question practices that have become second nature to you, as they may not be as effective as they once were.

Respect students and respond accordingly. As you give respect to them, they will likely give it back to you.

Smile when your students surprise you with a novel response or a kind gesture toward another classmate. Unspoken messages like smiles are often more potent than words.

Take time to enjoy life's small gifts with your students: the first snowfall, colored leaves in autumn, the first flower in the spring, a rainbow.

Use what you know about your students as you plan learning activities.

Validate every student at least once a week. Greet students by name, discover their interests, ask them to help you, and notice their efforts.

Write and wonder often, and bask in the glow of your students' learning capabilities.

e**X**pect that all students will succeed, as under your guidance, they are likely to do so.

Yearn to make your classroom an exciting place in which to learn and live.

Zero in on those learning activities that actively involve students and cause them to want to return to your classroom tomorrow.

Part I
Activities to Help Students Grow With Others

Activity 1

Grate Misteaks

Most students are too aware of their own mistakes. Not all children, however, realize that adults are just as mistake-prone as young people. Even more surprising is the discovery that mistakes have led to the invention of products, ideas, and tools that are integral parts of our daily lives.

Using the mistaken inventions of cheese, Velcro, chocolate chip cookies, and Silly Putty, or reading about famous people like J. K. Rowling, Albert Einstein, Rosa Parks, and Steven Spielberg, take your students on an excursion into the "Land of Oops"—the place where accidental discoveries turn into amazing creations. People who are now well known are so because they believed that "if at first you don't succeed, try, try again." Then, in an effort to help students appreciate both the inevitability and the benefits of making mistakes, join them in creating a bulletin board to revisit and reassess some of their most embarrassing moments.

Learning Objectives

Through this activity, students will:
- think critically and creatively,
- recognize the value of mistakes in the creative process,
- find humor in their own and others' mistakes,
- understand that mistakes are inevitable and acceptable, and
- tell and write personal anecdotes.

23

Materials

- Handout 1.1: Students' Grate Misteaks
- Handout 1.2: My Gratest Misteak
- Handout 1.3: Major League Mistakes
- Paper bag or pillowcase containing a chocolate chip cookie, a piece of Silly Putty, a Frisbee, a can of Coca-Cola, and a packet of sticky notes
- Pencils, colored pencils, pens, crayons, or markers
- Optional: *Mistakes That Worked* by Charlotte Foltz Jones and/or *Fantastic Failures* by Luke Reynolds (or another children's book about the benefits of mistake-making)
- For Classroom Extensions: *Be a Perfect Person in Just Three Days!* by Stephen Manes

Time

One 45-minute session

Activity Steps

1. Ask students to complete this statement: *The greatest inventor of all time is _____* . You can expect answers ranging from Marie Curie, Albert Einstein, George Washington Carver, and Thomas Edison, to "the person who invented the computer" and "whoever thought up pizza." Tell students: *Good answers, but they're all wrong!* (You may share a wry smile at this point, so students don't take you too seriously.) Then, reveal the answer, attributed to author Mark Twain, that the greatest inventor of all time is "accident."

2. Your students will probably look puzzled, so go on to prove your point with this story: *It was a long, hot day and a long, hot ride. The camel had bad breath and great aim when he spat at his rider, who rode along uncomfortably on his shifting, jerky perch. It's a good thing the traveler had milk in his animal-stomach pouch to quench his thirst. However, when he opened the pouch to drink some milk, a funny thing had happened. Can you guess what it was?* Don't be surprised if several students get the answer right: The milk had turned into cheese. The shaking up and down of the milk, coupled with the enzymatic action of the animal-stomach pouch, curdled the milk.

3. Discuss inventions that resulted from mistakes. Take out your bag or pillowcase of inventions. Read some or all of the following descriptions. As students guess what each invention was, pull out the item for all to see. These inventions are also described in the book *Mistakes That Worked* (Jones, 2016).

- **Invention 1:** Ruth Wakefield was running around trying to clean and cook for the guests staying at her inn in Massachusetts when she realized she'd forgotten to make a dessert for dinner. "No problem," she thought. "I'll make chocolate cookies." She searched her kitchen for baking chocolate (the dark, bitter kind), but all she had were milk chocolate candy bars. She hurriedly broke up the candy bars and tossed the pieces into the cookie dough. What did Ruth Wakefield invent? (Chocolate chip cookies.)

- **Invention 2:** During World War II, real rubber was scarce, so the U.S. government asked scientists to invent artificial rubber. James Wright experimented with silicone and boric acid, but all he got was a lump of stuff that was too flexible and bouncy to be made into tires or army boots. He thought he had failed completely. Several years later, Peter Hodgson saw the advantages of Wright's "failed" experiment. What very silly thing had James Wright invented? (Silly Putty.)

- **Invention 3:** In Bridgeport, CT, there was a bakery known for its delicious pies. Each pie came baked in its own metal dish. Students at nearby Yale University loved these pies—and the dishes. When the students were done eating, they had a toy. They'd toss the pie dish from person to person in an odd game of catch. Whoever threw the pie dish called out the name of the bakery imprinted on it. What was the name of the bakery and the toy? (Frisbee.)

- **Invention 4:** Dr. John Pemberton invented a hair dye and a couple of potions that made people go to the toilet more, or less, often. While he was formulating a medicine to get rid of nervousness and headaches, he decided it needed a little water and ice. By accident, his assistant added the wrong water—carbonated instead of from the tap. What did Dr. Pemberton and his assistant invent? (Coca-Cola.)

- **Invention 5:** A large manufacturer needed a really strong glue to compete with super glue. One scientist had the almost perfect formula, but his glue was too weak to hold anything together permanently. Four years later, another scientist from the same company was singing in a church choir. He kept losing his place in the hymnal as all of his page markers fell to the floor. It was then that he thought of the weak glue, and a great way to use it. What new product did the scientists invent? (Sticky notes.)

4. Once you have shared the vignettes, ask students to explain the point of these stories. Example responses: *A mistake isn't always a bad thing if you view it in a different way. Sometimes you have to make mistakes before you learn something new.*

5. Talk about personal mistakes. Tell your students about a mistake in your own life or an embarrassing moment that you'll never forget. (Once, one of this book's authors, Jim, had just finished telling his fourth graders to be sure to choose *only* dry-erase markers to use on the new, white marker boards. Within 10 minutes, Jim had covered an entire marker board with sentences and diagrams *using a permanent black marker.*) Ask students if they've ever made a mistake that left them feeling silly or embarrassed. You might ask:

   - Did you ever score a goal or basket for the other team? What happened? How did you feel?
   - Did you ever talk to someone you thought was your friend, only to find out you were talking to a total stranger? What happened? How did you feel?
   - Did you ever put your clothes on inside out, or underdress for an occasion? What happened? How did you feel?
   - Did you ever say something behind a teacher's or a relative's back, only to discover that the person heard you? What happened? How did you feel?
   - Did you ever make a mistake that turned out not to be a mistake after all? What happened? How did you feel?

6. Allow several volunteers to tell their stories. Once the laughter subsides, ask: *What did you learn from your mistakes?* Next, explain that the class is going to compile a bulletin board called "Our Gratest Misteaks" (misspelled on purpose, of course!), in which students (and the teacher) reveal some of their most embarrassing moments.

7. Write about mistakes. Display or distribute Handout 1.1: Students' Grate Misteaks. Read the descriptions of mistakes and discuss them together. Then, using Handout 1.2: My Gratest Misteak, have students write and, if they wish, illustrate their greatest mistake. If students have trouble thinking of their own mistakes, suggest that they write about one made by a family member. Caution students against revealing anything too personal or embarrassing.

8. Display stories about mistakes. Post the written accounts, including your own, for all to see. You have just taught your students a lifelong lesson: Mistakes happen to everyone, and people can often learn something from them.

Classroom Extensions

- Using Handout 1.3: Major League Mistakes as a springboard, have students research the mistakes and setbacks of famous people. The website Wanderlust Worker (https://wanderlustworker.com/48-famous-failures-who-will-inspire-you-to-achieve) highlights the struggles and eventual triumphs of people as diverse as Abraham Lincoln, Beyoncé, Dr. Seuss, Colonel Sanders, and Katy Perry. You may have to pick and choose among these "famous failures," depending on the maturity level of your students, but the case is clear: Even very well-known people had some bumps along the way.

- Have students write letters to parents, business and community leaders, and state or national figures asking them what important mistakes they made in their lives and what they learned from them. Students can write or talk about what the mistakes were and how they affected the people's lives.

- Read the book *Be a Perfect Person in Just Three Days!* as a class or view the video (https://www.youtube.com/watch?v=SCL8BHz8SFg). This is a hilarious set of misadventures attempted by a young boy for whom looking good and being right was essential. Have a discussion about the stress caused when someone strives to be perfect. Depending upon the maturity level of your students, consider expanding this discussion into ways in which kids feel pressured in school.

School Extension

Take a photograph of each teacher and staff member. Post these headshots on a bulletin board, next to descriptions of memorable mistakes these adults made in life. Students will thoroughly enjoy having adults humanized in this way.

Family Extension

On open house night, ask parents and other visitors to anonymously write down mistakes they've made in their lives, using Handout 1.2: My Gratest Misteak. The next day, have students read the visitors' responses and post these embarrassing (but fun) moments on a bulletin board.

Variations

- Compile mistakes (anonymous, if you choose) on your classroom or school website or in individual or class booklets.
- Encourage students to use a small notebook to keep a "Learning Log" in which they record mistakes that have either turned out not to be mistakes or have taught students something good or important. At the end of the year, have an informal sharing of these "grate misteaks."

Handout 1.1
Students' Grate Misteaks

Here are some fifth and sixth graders' grate misteaks. What do you think these students learned from their misteaks?

My feet fell asleep in the band room, and every time I stood up, I fell down!

I got some sand in my bathing suit while I was riding waves in the ocean. I pulled my bathing suit down to get the sand out—and then I came to my senses when the waves retreated and I was left with my swim trunks down by my knees.

Once I put a can of Coke in the freezer thinking it was the refrigerator. The Coke blew up all over everything.

HANDOUT 1.1, continued

One time I was leaning back on a chair with one foot under the TV. I leaned back too far, and the TV went through the wall in my bedroom.

My dad and I always punch each other softly. I went up to this guy who looked like my dad and I started punching him in the stomach. Luckily, just softly, because he wasn't my dad.

One day I was running away from the lawn sprinkler so I wouldn't get wet, and I ran right into my little brother's wading pool!

My brother put pancakes in the microwave, but rather than cook them for 2 minutes, he pressed an extra zero. They blew up. (So did my mom.)

Handout 1.2
My Gratest Misteak

Here's the mistake I made:_____
_____
_____
_____
_____

Here's what I learned: _____
_____
_____
_____
_____

This mistake actually turned out okay when: _____
_____
_____
_____
_____
_____
_____

_____
_____

Handout 1.3
Major League Mistakes

Directions: Even the most successful people make mistakes. When they do, there is almost always something to be learned from the mistake. Read and respond to the following examples.

The greatest quarterbacks complete only 60% of their passes. The best basketball players make only about 50% of their shots. Most major league baseball players get on base only about 25% of the time.

What do you think these major leaguers learned from their mistakes?

Top oil companies, even with the help of expert geologists, must dig an average of 10 wells before finding oil.

What do you think the geologists and other experts learned from their mistakes?

Producers at the first television station that hired Oprah Winfrey tried to give her a makeover and turn her into a beauty queen instead of a reporter. It didn't work. Oprah didn't fit this fake version of herself—and she didn't want to. However, the station had a contract stating that Winfrey could not be fired, so the producers assigned her to a local morning show called *People Are Talking*. It was the beginning of Oprah's incredibly successful career as a talk show host.

What do you think the television producers learned from their mistake?

Publishers rejected J. K. Rowling's first Harry Potter book more than 25 times. Dr. Seuss's first book was rejected by 27 publishers. He was going home to burn it in his fireplace when a friend he met on the way home asked if he could give it to another friend who published children's books. More than 60 books later, everyone knows Dr. Seuss.

What do you think the publishers learned from their mistakes? How did these authors respond to their initial rejections?

Activity 2

I Wanna Be Bugged by You

At the beginning of the school year, students may not be familiar with their classmates or teachers. This activity allows everyone to get to know one another a little better from the inside out. As students write their answers to questions related to important aspects of their lives, they open windows to their interests, abilities, goals, and dreams. Displayed as a centipede with many parts, students' personal stories combine to show both the diversity and the commonalities of their classmates.

Learning Objectives

Through this activity, students will:
- identify and write about their personal strengths, interests, and goals;
- identify significant people in their lives and explore why these individuals are important;
- think critically and creatively about the lives they have led, the lives they are leading, and the lives they will lead in the future; and
- review and ask questions about their peers' work.

Materials

- Handout 2.1: Bug Myself
- Handout 2.2: A Sampling of Bug Parts
- Colored construction paper (one sheet per student)
- Scissors
- Crayons, markers, or paints
- Paste, glue, or tape

Time

One 45-minute session

Activity Steps

1. Ask students if they know what it means to "bug" someone. Confirm that it means to pester or bother the person. Then say: *Sometimes we might bug someone in a friendly way—not to bother them or upset them, but to get to know them a little better. That's what we'll do today: We'll bug each other just enough to learn a little more about everyone in our class.*

2. Tell students that they are going to write about themselves and then share what they've written, first with another student and then with the whole class (optional).

3. Display or distribute Handout 2.1: Bug Myself. Read it with students and explain that they should choose one of the situations to write about. Take a few minutes to offer your own take on one of the four situations or, if you team teach, ask a teammate or two to respond orally to one.

4. Distribute Handout 2.2: A Sampling of Bug Parts. Read the entries together, briefly discussing what readers learn from the writers' ideas. Allow 10–20 minutes for students to draft their responses. Gauge the time as you circulate among students, being sensitive to those who need encouragement and just a bit more time to develop their thoughts.

5. Have each student pair up with another in the classroom. Ask partners to read one another's responses and bug each other by asking questions to help clarify or elaborate on ideas. After a few minutes of discussion, have students work individually again to refine their responses.

6. After each student has written an acceptable second (or third) draft, distribute single sheets of colored construction paper and have students write

their final drafts. (*Note.* If you are using the activity with more than one classroom, we suggest using a different color of construction paper for each room.) Suggest that students round off the corners of the sheet so that the shape is more oval, like a centipede's body segment. Or, you may decide to let your class's centipede take a changing shape dependent on students' different writing formats.

7. When they finish writing, give students additional construction paper and invite them to add feet of their own unique design to their centipede part, placing their first name on one foot and their last name on the other. Students may also wish to decorate their bug parts and feet further, with glitter, feathers, or other fun materials.

8. Create and display the bug. Hang the written bug parts on a large wall, connected to approximate the body of a centipede. Inevitably, students will soon call this bug by some name they've invented!

For Surefire Success

Introducing this activity by telling your own story will heighten your students' interest. Many students will be eager to learn about what you might have been instead of a teacher, or whom you would invite to dinner if you could invite anyone at all. As an added bonus, students will see that they can choose to answer seriously, rather than jokingly, if they wish.

Classroom Extensions

- Ask for volunteers to create a large "bug head" to lead the parade of bug body parts. The ones we create are usually made from large poster board, using Styrofoam balls (cut in half) for the eyes; glitter and glue for the nose, mouth, and rosy cheeks; and pipe cleaners for antennas and eyelashes.
- Keep the bug's head displayed all year but ask students to create different body parts in response to different prompts. Examples:
  o If you could live in the past, present, or future, which would you choose, and why?
  o The President has asked you to lead a special commission on school improvement. What are some of the topics you'd like to address?

Family Extension

Complete this activity during the first few weeks of school, making sure it is available for view during open house. This assignment is a tremendous hit with parents.

Variation

This is an excellent activity to do with large groups of students. For example, if you team teach with three other teachers, introduce the activity to all students at once. Then distribute construction paper, by color, to individual homerooms or classrooms. When the single large bug is posted for all to see, mix the colors; students can then read and identify their teammates' responses by homeroom or classroom.

Handout 2.1
Bug Myself

Directions: Read the following four "buggy ideas." Then choose and write about one of the ideas.

You are allowed to invite three people, living or dead, to your home for dinner. They might be famous people, or they might be people from your personal family history. By writing about whom you will invite and why you will invite them, you'll be telling us something about the kinds of things and people you enjoy.

You are about to turn 100 years old and are writing your life's story. It might even be turned into a movie! By writing about what you have done in your life, you'll be telling us about the goals and dreams you have for your future.

You have been granted three wishes: one for you, one for your family, and one for the Earth. By revealing your three wishes and why they are important to you, you'll be telling us about what you value most for yourself and others.

Someone has decided to hire you for a job. Describe what the job is and why you are perfectly suited to do it. In this way, you'll tell us about your strengths and your interests.

Handout 2.2
A Sampling of Bug Parts

Read what some "bugged" fourth-grade students wrote about themselves.

If someone hired me to do a job, I would choose to be a chemist because I love math and science, and I'm really good at them. I also like mixing and making new things. This job would also be good for me because I'm not afraid to make mistakes. If I would make a mistake, I would just keep trying until I got things right, and if I still couldn't get things right, I would ask for help. The last reason I would like to be a chemist is because I think they make a lot of money, don't they?

If I could invite anyone to eat dinner with me, living or dead, I would invite my real grandma, because she died before I was born. Everyone tells me that I look just like her when I don't even know who she is. I would also invite my third-grade teacher, Miss Heflin, because she retired during the school year because of a heart problem. Lastly, I'd invite my new cousin, Eric James, because I would like to get to know him as if he were my brother. The reason I chose him was that I only have one other cousin, and he is not allowed to do anything that will get him hyper. So, I'd like to have another cousin to play football and games with (I'm an only child).

If I had to invite three people to dinner, I would invite my mother because she died when I was 5, and I would like to meet her again. I would also invite Walt Disney because I would like to meet the man who gave us Mickey Mouse and so many other wonderful characters. And last but not least, I would invite Michelle Obama, because I'd like to ask her what it was like to live in the White House and if she personally helped with the vegetable garden.

Now that I'm 100 years old, here's what I've done with my life. I became a best-selling author because I love to write, and I didn't have to work at it 24 hours a day, only when I had an idea. This still gave me time for my kids. When I wasn't writing or watching my kids, I trained my pets and other people's pets. All of these things kept me so busy that I didn't have time to cook or do the laundry, so my husband had to do those things. I retired when I was 70, moved in with my youngest child, and played with their children all day.

Activity 3

ABCs of Our Lives

All students are familiar with alphabet books, although many may think of them as books for very young children. Challenge this concept by inviting your students to research their personal histories, think introspectively, and fashion their discoveries into autobiographies in an ABC format.

For student wordsmiths, graphic designers, and visual artists alike, this is a stimulating activity that affords both self-exploration and self-expression. It also offers an opportunity for children to reminisce with their families about important events and people in their lives.

Learning Objectives

Through this activity, students will:
- identify significant people and events in their lives,
- plan and carry out a project over several days,
- write creatively within an assigned framework, and
- review and edit their peers' work.

Materials

- Handout 3.1: Four Ways to Make a Book
- Handout 3.2: Alphabetical Me
- Handout 3.3: My ABC Book
- Handout 3.4: The ABCs of Editing

- Several ABC books
- Materials for making books (see Handout 3.1: Four Ways to Make a Book)
- Dictionaries and thesauruses
- Colored pencils, pens, crayons, or markers

Time

One 40-minute session to introduce the activity; additional at-home and in-school time to complete it

Preparation

Select one or two alphabet books to serve as an introduction to the entire lesson. We love these: *P is for Pterodactyl: The Worst Alphabet Book Ever*, *A is for Artichoke: A Foodie Alphabet From Artichoke to Zest*, and *The Weighty Word Book*. If you can't locate any of these books, consider one of your personal favorites or find one in your school library. The more familiar you are with the book ahead of time, the more excitement will be generated as you inspire your students to become actively involved in this activity. If possible, select additional alphabet books for students to peruse. Try to find examples that are designed, written, and illustrated in a variety of ways. For example, some books rely on illustrations, while others use single words or paragraphs to get their messages across. Plan to keep these books in the classroom so that students may look at them during the course of the activity.

After you have reviewed Handout 3.1: Four Ways to Make a Book, determine what types of book-making options you wish to have available for your students. Assemble the materials specified for these types of books.

Activity Steps

1. Before showing any books, ask students to share their own ideas about alphabet books. You might ask questions such as:
   - What do alphabet books try to do?
   - How do the words and art communicate messages to the reader?
   - Do you have a favorite alphabet book? Why do you like it so much?

2. Read portions of one or two of your favorite ABC books with students. Provide specific details about what you like about these books. You might

also wish to highlight a few other alphabet books you've located by providing a very brief overview of each one. The main goal during this initial contact with alphabet books is to have students recognize the power that these books have to convey specific messages. Point out that alphabet books might do one of several things, including:

- focus on one main idea or topic,
- incorporate a rhythmic pattern (such as alliteration or rhyme), or
- rely heavily on illustrations to communicate the main idea to the reader.

Tell students that they will be looking at and discussing other alphabet books in preparation for creating their own personal books.

3. Have students explore ideas in small groups. Depending upon the number of books you have, divide the class into groups of 2–4 students to examine one or two alphabet books. Allow about 10 minutes for students to review the books and identify:

- the way the authors have used the alphabet, and
- the element of the book that the group likes the most (e.g., illustration, rhyming verse, alliteration).

4. Share ideas in the large group. Have one person from each group describe the group's books and the primary method the authors used to communicate ideas to the reader. Be sure to highlight instances in which the authors used words and phrases effectively to paint a picture for the readers.

5. Challenge students to describe their life in an alphabet format. Distribute Handout 3.2: Alphabetical Me and Handout 3.3: My ABC Book, and review the directions together. Students should understand how to embellish each of the letters for their alphabet books. They won't merely write "B is for Beach"; rather, they will take it a step further and explain how "B is for Beach" identifies something important to them. Some additional examples might be helpful to share:

- B is for the Beach—any Beach. I just love the salt, air, and water.
- T is for the Train I ride to school with my mom, who rides to work on the subway every day.
- L is for Love: for Laughter, Long walks, Lullabies, Litter cleanup, the Library, and Lunch. These are all things I enjoy with the people I Love.

6. This activity is not one that can (or should) be completed during one session. Rather, allow time both in the classroom and at home for students to complete this activity over several days. If students get stuck trying to figure out the particular personal meaning for a letter, encourage them to ask close friends or family members to offer some advice. Also, remind stu-

dents to use the dictionary and thesaurus to find more unusual words for their personal alphabet books.

7. Confer with students as needed. Throughout the process of creating ABC books, you will need to confer with students individually to be sure that they have a grasp on the format and on your expectations. Often, students might need a specific suggestion for a letter or an idea that doesn't seem to take shape. The following might be helpful:

   • It will be natural for students to shape each letter into a very simple thought, such as: "A is for Ann, my middle name." Encourage children to expand upon a simple phrase: "A is for Ann, my middle name—a name my grandmother gave me."

   • Even though the book will be written in ABC order, suggest that students jump around from letter to letter, working first with those letters for which an idea comes quickly.

   • Help students see ways to reshape ideas to fit certain letters. For example, if a student has already used the word "math" to go with the letter M, suggest for S: "S is for school, a place where I really enjoy math class."

   • Encourage students to be creative about using letters such as X and Z: "X is part of tic-tac-toe, which my uncle and I play while I wait for my allergy shot." "X is the railroad X-ing by every day on the bus." "Z is an N turned NiNety degreeZ, which is the temperature I like best!"

8. Have students pair up with others in the classroom, offering both positive feedback and constructive criticism. Display or distribute Handout 3.4: The ABCs of Editing and explain that partners should use the ideas presented to guide them as they review one another's writing. This will help students edit and refine their ideas. It will also allow them to consider suggestions about those letters for which they still need inspiration. Through this peer review process, students will learn that creativity and problem solving benefit from collaboration with others.

9. Have students turn their ABC statements into ABC books. It may be helpful for you to present a few specific ideas to help students decide upon a format. For example, some students may feel that a picture book will work best, while others may like to design a fold-out poster book or a flip book.

10. Once students have determined a format for their work, have them proceed with their final copies. Because students have worked so hard up to this point, stress that they should take the time to show off their ideas in a creative and colorful way.

Classroom Extension

Once the books are bound, have an alphabet book reading party so that students have an opportunity to share their books and to read those of their peers. You might also wish to arrange for the books to be displayed in the media center, or you might send some to the principal to read.

Family Extension

Plan an alphabet book reading party for families. Include punch and cookies along with the readings to give the party the flavor of a library or bookstore event. Have students design their own business cards (as authors, poets, artists, or designers) to distribute during the reading party.

Handout 3.1
Four Ways to Make a Book

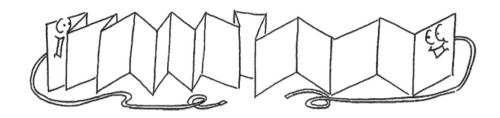

I. Fold-Out Book

Here's what you need:

> Several sheets of construction paper of equal sizes
> Tape
> Yarn

Here's what to do:

1. Arrange the pages in a row.
2. Tape the pages together and fold them accordion-style.
3. Unfold the pages and tape yarn to the back of the opened book. To close the book, fold it again and tie the yarn in front.

Suggestions:

> Make a group book for which each person contributes a page.
> Make a wordless picture book.
> Make pocket pages: Cut sheets of construction paper in half. Tape the half sheets to each page, leaving the top open to form a pocket. Use the pockets to hold quarter-page sheets that tell or expand on the story of the large page.

II. Shape Book

Here's what you need:

> Construction paper for the book's cover
> Plain or lined paper for the book's pages
> Paper punch and yarn **or** stapler
> Scissors

Here's what you do:

1. Place sheets of plain or lined paper between two pieces of construction paper.
2. Sew or staple the book together along the left-hand side.
3. On the book's front cover, draw an outline of the desired shape. The sewn or stapled book edge should stay within the outline.
4. Cut along the outline, making sure the binding remains intact.

Suggestions:

> Use a shape that represents the subject of the book.
> Ask students to predict from the shape what the book will be about.

III. Softcover Book

Here's what you need:

> Sheets of plain paper (8 1/2" x 11"; using both sides of the paper, one sheet makes eight book pages)
> Needle and thread
> Scissors or butter knife
> Construction paper, wallpaper, or cloth for the book's cover
> Glue

Here's what you do:

1. Stack the sheets of plain paper evenly and fold them in half. Fold them in half a second time.
2. With needle and thread, sew the pages along the second fold. To do this, start at the middle of the folded edge and stitch up to the top edge; then stitch all the way down to the bottom edge; then stitch back up to the middle. Tie off the thread ends.
3. Use scissors or a butter knife to slit the remaining folded page edges.
4. Cut the paper or cloth for the cover so its size is 5 1/2" x 8 1/2". Glue the cover to the front- and back-facing pages.

IV. Hardcover Book

Here's what you need:

> › Sheets of plain paper (8 1/2" x 11"; using both sides of the paper, one sheet makes four book pages)
> › Needle and thread
> › Wallpaper or wrapping paper for cover
> › Two sheets cardboard, such as shirt cardboard (at least 9 1/2" x 6 1/2")
> › Glue
> › Two sheets (8 1/2" x 5 3/8") construction paper

Here's what you do:

1. Stack the sheets of plain paper evenly and fold them in half.
2. With needle and thread, sew the pages along the fold, 1/8" from the folded edge. (If you wish, you can use a sewing machine to stitch the pages. This is a good technique if you want to mass-produce the books.)
3. Cut wallpaper or wrapping paper about 2 inches larger than the open book on all sides.
4. Cut each sheet of cardboard a little larger than a single book page. Place the cardboard sheets on the wrong side of the wallpaper or wrapping paper, leaving a 1/4" space for the book's spine. Glue and fold the corners and edges of the cover to the cardboard, as shown.
5. Glue the front-facing page, spine, and back-facing page to the cardboard side (inside) of the cover, as shown.
6. Glue construction paper to inside front and back covers.
7. Close the book to ensure proper folding. Let it dry.

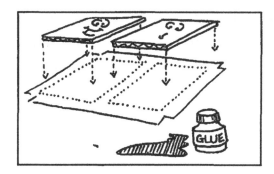

51

Handout 3.2
Alphabetical Me

Directions: Use the alphabet to describe and explain different things about yourself. You will need to think creatively and carefully about the important people and events in your life so that your responses reflect the person you are, the people you know, and the things you like to do. Using just a word or two is not enough. You need to use phrases that describe and explain what you want your reader to understand about you.

Once you have completed and edited your alphabet, you will use what you have written to create your personal ABC book.

A Few Reminders

» Be sure that each entry relates directly to you.

» Be careful in selecting words.
Example: B is for Brian, ~~that~~ who is my oldest brother. ("That" is incorrect; "who" is correct.)

» Be sure you have included descriptive details.
Examples without <u>enough detail</u> include:
- **A** is for athletics, a fun thing. (This does not tell anything about you.)
- **M** is for movies, which I love. (This does not tell enough about you.)
- **C** is for Carla, my oldest sister. (This does not tell why Carla is important to you.)

» **Instead, write phrases that provide more detail:**
- **A** is for athletics, which I enjoy. Basketball is my favorite sport.
- **M** is for movies, which I love—all kinds, but especially scary ones.
- **C** is for Carla, my oldest sister, who loves tennis and always helps me with my homework.

NAME:_____ DATE:_____

Handout 3.3
My ABC Book

A	
B	
C	
D	
E	
F	
G	
H	
I	
J	
K	
L	

HANDOUT 3.3, continued

M	
N	
O	
P	
Q	
R	
S	
T	
U	
V	
W	
X	
Y	
Z	

Handout 3.4
The ABCs of Editing

By Yourself

1. Reread your entries. Place an asterisk (*) next to three statements that you really love. These are the ones of which you are the proudest.
2. Place a question mark (?) next to those letters that still need statements or, in your opinion, need better or different statements.
3. Place a dash (–) next to three items that you will agree to change.

With Your Partner

4. Exchange papers and read each other's ABCs without making any comments or asking any questions.
5. Discuss the entries together. Ask questions if an entry is not clear to you. Offer praise for statements that you really like.
6. Reread the items in your partner's paper that have a question mark (?) or dash (–) next to them. Write down any ideas you have that might help the writer edit these statements. Can you suggest details or words that will make the entry more interesting, moving, or fun?

By Yourself

7. Take back your ABC statements from your partner. Look again at those entries you have marked with a dash (–). Concentrate on reworking these entries so that the language sparkles.

8. Go back to the items highlighted with a question mark (?). Read the suggestions your partner wrote and make any changes you think will improve your statements.

With Your Partner

9. Share your rewritten statements.
10. Work together to help each other finalize all entries.

By Yourself

11. Put the finishing touches on your writing!

Activity 4

Little Stories of Our Classroom

Within your classroom walls, there are hundreds of stories waiting to be told. This lesson provides an opportunity to give voice to some of those stories. As students write and share their personal ideas and experiences, they'll gain an appreciation for the special characteristics that make up the many personalities in their classroom. They'll also recognize that their classmates' diverse traits and histories combine into a cohesive unit with its own unique collective personality. Additionally, they may find some things they have in common with others that were previously unknown. The resulting class biography is an excellent project to complete before an open house or parent conferences. The completed books are well received by parents.

Learning Objectives

Through this activity, students will:
- identify similarities and differences among students in the class,
- recognize that there is more to people than what is seen on the surface,
- tell their personal stories orally,
- interview one another and write one another's personal stories, and
- review and edit their peers' writing.

Materials

- Handout 4.1: The Me I'd Like Others to See
- Handout 4.2: I'd Like to Get to Know You
- Materials for making books (see Handout 3.1: Four Ways to Make a Book)
- Dictionaries and thesauruses
- Pens, crayons, or markers
- For Classroom Extension: Camera for photos and/or videos

Time

Two 40-minute sessions; additional in-school time to assemble the class book

Activity Steps

1. Explain to students that they will be working together to write a classroom "history" book: a compilation of brief stories about everyone in the classroom. Instead of writing about themselves, students will interview and write about each other.

2. On the board, draw a line and make two columns, titled "Same" and "Different." Ask students to look around the room at their classmates and share specific characteristics that make them similar (e.g., all attend the same school; they're all wearing shoes) as well as those that make them different (e.g., gender, height, or hair color). List these in their respective columns.

3. Distribute Handout 4.1: The Me I'd Like Others to See. Review the questions together and ask students to complete the handout while you do the same. For item 2, help students understand that they should describe a specific characteristic or trait about themselves, or an interesting aspect about their life (e.g., "I have lived in four states and gone to five schools."). For item 5, explain that students should write a specific piece of information about themselves that they believe is important for others to know (e.g., "I am an animal lover and hope to be a veterinarian someday.").

4. After approximately 5–10 minutes, share with students the "secrets" you have written about yourself. Ask for volunteers to share several of their ideas also.

5. Define and talk about assumptions. Discuss how people form opinions and ideas about others even when they don't know them well. You might ask questions such as:
   - What does it mean to make an assumption?
   - Why do we assume things about people? Can making assumptions be good . . . bad . . . both?
   - Why don't we always know what a person is really like?
   - Why is it worthwhile to learn more about people? What are some ways to do this?

6. Make the point that sometimes people don't take the time to find out what a person is really like. Many times, they think about people in terms of what is most obvious about them: their actions, behaviors, even the clothes they wear. Then ask: *What makes us a special class?*

7. Continue with a discussion centering on the notion that it is the collective similarities and differences among students that make each class unique.

8. Explain that students will work in pairs and will share more about themselves. Distribute Handout 4.2: I'd Like to Get to Know You. Review it with students, explaining that partners can use this sheet as they interview one another. Encourage partners to ask their own questions about the responses, too, to gather additional information about each other. Interviewers may want to focus on only one or two ideas or ask questions about all of the ideas. Make sure students understand that they will use the information they acquire to write about their partner.

9. Give an example for item 2 on the handout, such as being musical. By asking several of the questions listed, the interviewer may discover that the classmate they are interviewing comes from a family of musicians. Or, the interviewer may find that the classmate can play three instruments and wants to learn to play even more. The more probing that is done, the more complete the final responses can be as the interviewer writes about the interviewee.

10. Allow 15–20 minutes for this step of the activity. Remind students of the time remaining halfway through and again when there are approximately 3 minutes remaining.

11. Have students write independently about the people they interviewed. Before they begin, share a few of the following "little stories" written by our fifth-grade students. Focus attention on how the stories are written: They are specifically about the unique characteristics of each individual, they are brief, and they are to the point.

- Jeannette is a French girl filled with forgiveness and kindness. She is very generous and smart, and her smile makes you happy. She'll never turn you away if you want to talk or you have a problem to solve.
- Patrick is the hilarious type, always making you happy when you're gloomy and happier when you're already in a good mood. Patrick is smart, a good actor, and best of all, my friend.
- Elena is a smiley person. She laughs, giggles, and acts as if she's having a ball. In academics she's under control, a very good student, and doesn't know the meaning of "being upset" because she never gets that way.
- Maruf is a good cartoonist—he makes up characters and gives them names and personalities! He is very smart and a whiz at the computer. I like him a lot. He makes me happy.

12. Have students use the information obtained during their interviews to construct their pieces of writing. You might wish to specify the minimum number of sentences.

13. Have peers review and edit the stories. Have students divide into pairs, this time with a different partner than the person they interviewed. Explain that these pairs will act as peer editors to help revise one another's writing. Encourage students to bring their stories to life by using descriptive words rather than dull words like *nice*, *pretty*, or *fun*. Remind them to use the thesauruses you've provided to diversify their word choice and the dictionaries to check spelling and word meanings.

14. Once the revisions are completed, have students meet with their original partners. Students should read the stories about themselves and let the writers know if the information is accurate. Allow time for students to work individually to put any finishing touches on their stories.

15. Once the stories are written in final form, decide together how to compile them into a book by discussing questions such as these:
    - Will we write the stories by hand or type them on the computer?
    - What size paper will we use?
    - How many stories will go on each page?
    - How will we illustrate the book?

    One idea is to ask for volunteers to draw caricatures of students. This is a wonderful opportunity for budding artists.

Classroom Extension

Following the completion of the writing, consider designing a bulletin board or hallway display that includes photos of students next to the short stories about them. This can be an especially appealing bulletin board at the beginning of the school year, when students are just getting to know one another.

School Extension

Send students to interview and write about other people in the school (e.g., the principal, secretary, custodian, teachers, other students) using Handout 4.2: I'd Like to Get to Know You.

Family Extensions

- Have students interview and write about members of their family.
- Suggest that students work with members of their families to create family books for which members interview and write about one another.

Variations

- Create a bulletin board display that uses silhouettes of students' heads with the stories written on index cards and taped or glued to the silhouettes.
- If your classroom has a website, post three or four student biographies per week so that parents get to know their child's classmates. You might also post your own biography.
- Have students prepare brief oral presentations about the people they interviewed. Record the presentations and combine them into a class audiobook or video, which can be shared at the end of the school year to note how people have changed and who has moved to another school.

Handout 4.1
The Me I'd Like Others to See

Directions: There are many things about each of us that others do not know. Some things we want to keep to ourselves, but other things we'd really like others in the class to know. Think about some things you'd like your classmates to know about you. Write your ideas below.

1. Most people don't know I am very interested in:_____

   _____

   _____

2. Most people don't know this about me:_____

   _____

   _____

3. Most people don't know that a hobby I enjoy is: _____

   _____

   _____

4. Three words to describe me are:_____

   _____

   _____

The one thing I would like everyone to know about me is:_____

_____

_____

_____

_____

NAME:_____ DATE:_____

I'd Like to Get to Know You

Directions: Use the questions on this sheet to help you learn more about your partner. If you think of other questions to ask, that's great!

Name of student I interviewed: _____

1. What is something that really interests you?

   Why does it interest you?

   How did you learn about it?

   Is someone else you know interested in it, too? What new things have you learned about this interest since you started exploring it?

   _____

   _____

   _____

   _____

2. What is a unique trait you have?

   What is something about you that's very special?

   How did you discover that about yourself?

   Does someone else you know have the same trait?

   How do you use the trait? Where? When?

   Why are you glad you have that trait?

   _____

   _____

   _____

   _____

   _____

HANDOUT 4.2, continued

3. What is something most people don't know about you that you'd like them to know?

   Does anyone at all know this about you?

   Why do you want people to know this about you?

   How do you think people will react when they learn this new thing about you?

   _____

   _____

   _____

   _____

   _____

   _____

   _____

4. What is a special hobby you enjoy?

   How did you get started on your hobby?

   Does someone else enjoy the hobby with you? Who?

   Why do you enjoy it so much?

   When do you do your hobby?

   How much time do you spend on it?

   What have you had to do to learn more about your hobby?

   _____

   _____

   _____

   _____

   _____

   _____

   _____

Activity 5

Box Up Your life

Students are often asked to tell a little about themselves to classmates, either through writing projects or oral presentations, which helps to build a sense of community among classmates. In this activity, students consider aspects of themselves and their lives that are most important to them. Then, they look for objects that symbolize each aspect. Finally, students assemble the objects into a boxed display—a "life box"—representative of themselves. You and your students will marvel at the variety of interests and expression this project inspires.

Learning Objectives

Through this activity, students will:
- identify personal characteristics, preferences, interests, feelings, and beliefs;
- recognize commonalities among themselves;
- think and work creatively to craft a personalized display box; and
- symbolize both abstract and concrete ideas.

Materials

- Handout 5.1: A Plan to Box Up My Life
- Empty shoebox (per student)
- Art materials for creating and decorating boxes (e.g., foam core, cardboard, glue, paints, wrapping paper)
- For Family Extension: Digital tool to film a video

Time

One 45-minute session to introduce the activity; additional at-home or in-class time to complete the boxes; 5 minutes per student for presentation of boxes

Preparation

This activity seems to work best when the teacher also shares a personally created life box, so we suggest that you construct yours ahead of time to share with students when you introduce the activity. Include a variety of aspects of yourself: physical traits that describe you, interests or hobbies, important beliefs, pivotal experiences, and goals. Deb prepared one decorated on the exterior with sea life wrapping paper to indicate her love of the ocean. Inside she placed a small dream catcher, a polished stone picked up in Ireland, a pen she had since she was a young writer, two photos of her family, an empty bag of M&Ms, and a book cover to share her favorite book.

Activity Steps

1. Ask students how they would describe the idea of "memory" to a creature from another planet who does not know the meaning of the word. Encourage students to respond in different ways by asking such questions as:
   - What picture, photograph, or image comes to your mind when you hear the word *memory*?
   - What color do you think memory is? Why?
   - Think of a very special memory of your own—it could be of an event, a person or something else. Can you think of one object that would best represent this memory if you wanted to share this memory with others?

2. Discuss ways to visually represent abstract concepts. Ask questions similar to these:
    *   What does friendship (or peace, or love) mean to you?
    *   What object could you use to show the concept of friendship (peace, love)?

3. Show students your life box and review how it uses objects to represent some of your memories as well as other characteristics about you. Explain to students that they will be using this idea of representing characteristics with objects in a creative project about their own lives. As you share your box, be specific about why you selected certain items and why you decorated your box as you did. Note to students that each of the objects in your life box is small enough to fit into a shoebox, no matter how big the memory may be; students, too, must follow this guideline.

4. Do personal brainstorming. Distribute Handout 5.1: A Plan to Box Up My Life, and have students independently brainstorm some characteristics, interests, feelings, beliefs, preferences, goals, or other things that make up what is most important in their lives. Be sure they include at least three abstract concepts, such as feelings, shared values, or personal traits. Here are a few starter ideas:
    *   feelings—love, excitement, confusion, joy, trust, hope, anticipation, closeness;
    *   shared values—religious faith, interest in politics, care for the environment, love of family;
    *   personal traits—musical, athletic, thoughtful, clever, different, jumpy, excitable; and
    *   hobbies and interests—photography, collecting baseball cards, pets, ice skating, music.

5. Next to each idea, students should write down a specific object or thing they could use to represent that aspect of themselves. For example, if a student chooses "joy" as a feeling, they might include a photograph of someone jumping off a diving board, or if a student selects "care for the environment," a small recycled object could be included. After brainstorming these ideas, have students mark with an asterisk (*) the 10 aspects of themselves that they consider to be the most creative and unique and that best represent them. These 10 items are the ones that will be included in their life boxes. Encourage students to include at least two abstract concepts.

6. Explain how to make, organize, and decorate the boxes. Encourage students to use their own ideas for both filling and decorating their life boxes.

As your students consider what to include and how to decorate their life boxes, offer these guidelines:

- Include at least 10 items that symbolize your most significant interests and personal characteristics.
- Plan and construct your box carefully so it's a complete and well-designed self-portrait.
- Decorate your box in a way that reflects something about yourself (e.g., cover it in wrapping paper with a balloon design to represent your love of celebrations).

7. Give a specific date when you want the life boxes to be completed and brought into class. Offer both an oral and a written reminder at least 2 days before the boxes are due.
8. Share the boxes in class. It is best to space out these presentations over several days so that everyone is attentive during the descriptions. We have found that three or four at one time seem to keep everyone's attention.

School Extension

Explain your project to your principal, another school administrator, another teacher, or other school personnel. Ask these individuals to prepare their own life boxes to share as a surprise to your students.

Family Extension

Record the presentations. Then, post the videos on your class website or play them while parents are arriving for open house or parent-teacher conferences.

Handout 5.1
A Plan to Box Up My Life

Directions: Use these categories to start construction of your life box. Add as many other categories as you wish.

HANDOUT 5.1, continued

Activity 6

A Personal Classroom Pledge

What better way to build community than by allowing students to cooperatively fashion a set of principles upon which they want their classroom to operate from day to day? In this activity, students take center stage, working first in small groups and then as an entire classroom to identify and agree on common classroom and personal goals. As you guide your students through this activity, you will foster teamwork, responsibility, decision making, and personal growth. At the same time, you will provide a hands-on experience in the democratic process.

Although the inspiration for this activity came from the U.S. Pledge of Allegiance, the activity is universal to democratic classrooms everywhere. Your personal classroom pledge can be the centerpiece for discussions of citizenship and democracy.

Learning Objectives

Through this activity, students will:
- work and think cooperatively toward a common goal,
- discuss and resolve issues related to classroom design and operation,
- understand the need for personal and social commitments, and
- experience a cooperative way to arrive at consensus.

Materials

- Handout 6.1: A Fifth-Grade Classroom Pledge
- Handout 6.2: Planning Our Pledge
- Newsprint or flipchart
- Markers
- One large sheet of poster board
- Dictionary and thesaurus
- Optional: Parchment paper and ribbon, or laminating material
- For Classroom Extension: *I Pledge Allegiance* by Pat Mora and Libby Martinez
- For Variation: *What Is the Constitution?* by Patricia Brennan Demuth

Time

Two 45-minute sessions

Background

The genesis for this lesson occurred in Jim's fourth-grade classroom one mid-November day. As the students were preparing for another day of class, they stood to make a rote recitation of the Pledge of Allegiance. Like millions of their schoolage counterparts across the U.S., the students droned on, looking at the ceiling, their friends, or blank space, attending 0% to the words they were reciting.

Jim had had it. "Stop!" he commanded in a voice not quite loud enough to be considered a shout, but with enough volume to put the kibosh on the morning's pledge.

"You can't stop us!" commented a shocked student, Michael. "It's the Pledge of Allegiance!"

At this point, Jim had the students sit down and do two things: (1) define the words *pledge* and *allegiance*, and (2) write the Pledge of Allegiance from start to finish.

The results, if nothing else, were informative and humorous. Every student mixed up at least one line in the pledge; only one student even came close to deciphering the word *indivisible*. The humor came in the form of a postscript from Rachel, who informed Jim that, until third grade, she thought the first line of the pledge was, "I led the pigeons to the flag." Because Rachel knew neither the word *pledge* nor *allegiance*, it made perfect sense to her to parade pigeons to the Stars and Stripes!

At this point, the idea of having students decipher the vocabulary and meaning of the Pledge of Allegiance and then create their own classroom pledge was born. After all, we reasoned, if students didn't understand the meaning behind a morning ritual they had been enacting for 4 years, then we needed to help them understand the importance of pledging—to both our country and their classroom. We recommend that you do this activity within the first month of school, if possible.

Activity Steps

1. Introduce the activity. Divide students into working groups of 4–5 students. Ask them to think of several things they would agree to this year in relation to:
   - school and schoolwork,
   - friendships,
   - families,
   - personal values,
   - the Earth and the environment, and
   - anything else important to them that doesn't fall under one of the first five categories.

2. Discuss and write pledges individually and in small groups. Display or distribute Handout 6.1: A Fifth-Grade Classroom Pledge. Ask students to comment on its contents—what makes sense to them, what sounds like something they believe, what sounds confusing, etc.

3. Using Handout 6.2: Planning Our Pledge, ask students to begin drafting each section of their personal classroom pledge individually, beginning each statement with the phrase "I promise . . ." followed by the commitments agreed upon by everyone in their group. Remind students to keep their individual promises short, similar to the examples from Handout 6.1. As students write, help them edit their thoughts and language into the simplest terms.

4. Once students have written their individual ideas, have them get together as groups and select one statement from each of the six categories that they would like to share with the entire class. Just like in a democracy, the statement with the majority of votes in each category will be presented to the class.

5. Discuss pledges with the whole class. Invite one member of each group to read the section on school and schoolwork. At the end of each group's recitation, ask the class: *Is there anyone in the class who cannot promise something that was just read?* If a student cites a specific objection, ask them

to elaborate on why the statement is not acceptable. Ask this student or others in the class if different wording would resolve the problem. If, after several minutes of discussion, you are not able to reach a compromise, drop the idea (at least for now) and move on to the next statement. For each group's statements, write on newsprint or a flipchart the general ideas or specific words upon which everyone agrees.

6. Continue this process through each of the six categories, allowing a different group to go first each time. Again, write down only those promises that all students say they can keep. If you skipped any categories, revisit them in hopes of finding unanimity for one statement. If none can be reached, drop this category from the classroom pledge.

7. Ask each group to elect one member of their initial work group to help complete the final editing of the classroom pledge. Allow this group of editors to take the classroom notes and compose a final draft of the ideas to which everyone has agreed. Tell the group to edit or rewrite the pages and prepare a clean copy of the edited pledge. Remind the group to use the dictionary to verify spellings or check the thesaurus for other words to use.

8. When the editors return, have them address the class with their revamped classroom pledge, making minor modifications as suggested by students.

9. When everyone has approved the final form of the pledge, type it on the upper two-thirds of a sheet of paper, leaving room for each student's signature at the bottom or on the sides in the margins, as seen in Handout 6.1. Post the pledge in your classroom and give a copy to each student.

10. Every morning after reciting the Pledge of Allegiance, join students in reciting their personal classroom pledge.

Classroom Extension

Ask students which parts of this activity were the most difficult. Odds are, they will mention the disagreements that arose in considering language and ideas for the pledge. Use this as a springboard to discuss the difficulties that families, communities, and businesses face every day. If you want to incorporate U.S. history into this discussion of the personal classroom pledge, consult *What Is the Constitution?*, which details the difficulties faced by the 55 original writers of one of the foundational documents of our nation.

Variation

In a whole-class setting, ask students to name, individually, some things they can promise in each of the six categories listed in Activity Step 1. Write each individual promise on the board. After 15–20 minutes, when there are no more suggestions to be made, ask students to close their eyes while you read each statement. Say: *If you cannot make this promise because you're afraid you can't keep it, raise your hand, and I'll erase that statement from the board. Only the items that are left at the end—the ones that everyone agrees to promise—will be included in our pledge.*

A fine supplement to this activity is to read aloud *I Pledge Allegiance*, a picture book that details how a girl and her Mexican-born grandmother are learning how to recite the Pledge flawlessly—Grandma Lobo, as she seeks citizenship, and granddaughter Libby for her daily classroom ritual in school.

Handout 6.1
A Fifth-Grade Classroom Pledge

As a member of Ms. Martinez's fifth-grade class, I promise to do all of these things to the best of my ability:

1. I promise not to steal or look in other people's private things.
2. I promise I will try to be honest.
3. I promise to compliment others whenever I can.
4. I promise to be aware of the world around me by helping to recycle in my classroom.
5. I promise to keep myself and others healthy by not spreading germs.
6. I promise to try to use my imagination whenever possible.

Signed this day, October 14, by:

Dominique   Alexander   Willis

JoMarie   Makiko

Pepe   Kristina   David

Latanya   Verremiah   Andrew

Trahn   Caitlin   B. Jo   Mary

Laurel   Rebecca   Josef   Bryan

Handout 6.2
Planning Our Pledge

Directions: Use this sheet to write notes about ideas for your classroom pledge. Later, you may also want to use it for writing and editing your group's statements.

Personal Values

The Earth and the Environment

Other Ideas

Activity 7

License to Be Me

Virtually every U.S. state allows its residents to order specially designed vanity plates—license plates that carry personalized letters and numbers. Kids love these one-of-a-kind license plates and the personal and (sometimes) cryptic messages many seem to carry. This activity taps into this cultural phenomenon, inviting students to use their knowledge, creativity, and humor to craft clever and expressive vanity plates of their own.

We use this activity during the first week of school, having students write their names on the back of their plates along with an explanation of why they created their specific slogan and design. Then we hang the plates on a clothesline in the classroom. (Our teacher license plate is HERE 4 U.) Later, students can attach the plates to their tables or desks.

Learning Objectives

Through this activity, students will:
- symbolize both abstract and concrete ideas,
- work creatively within a standard format, and
- consider their own unique traits and interests to design a license plate that displays these qualities.

Materials

- Handout 7.1: License Plates of the Rich and Famous (and Others, Too)
- Colored construction paper (one sheet per student)
- Scissors
- Crayons or markers
- Other decorative art materials

Time

One 45-minute session

Activity Steps

1. Ask students if anyone they know has a special license plate. If so, write the plates' letters and numbers on the board, and invite students to suggest what their messages might be.

2. If students don't know of any special plates, discuss other examples. Write some possible license plate messages and ask students who might own each plate. You can use ideas of your own, tap into the interests of your students, or use some of these:
   - EIEIO (a farmer, Old MacDonald)
   - HIGH CS (an opera singer, a sailor)
   - 1 PLUS 1 (a kindergarten teacher)
   - T 4 2 (a tap dancer, the queen of England)
   - ON R OL (an honors student)
   - OK 2 B U (psychologist)
   - 7 WE GUYZ (the Seven Dwarfs)
   - KITE KEY (Benjamin Franklin)
   - EZ DUZ IT (a tightrope walker)
   - FAM GUY (a proud dad)
   - BAT FAN 1 (A Batman fan)

3. Talk about symbolism. Explain to students that each of these plates symbolizes something important or fun to its owner. It might symbolize someone's appearance, personality or philosophy, accomplishments, or occupation. Remind students that symbolic ideas may be open to a wide range of meanings and interpretations.

4. By now, your students will be eager to get started designing their own vanity plates. Tell them to think of something unique about themselves: a personality trait, a goal, an activity they love, or anything that indicates who they are or what their lives are about. Share these guidelines:
   - Use any combination of letters or numbers, but no more than a total of seven (which is the limit for most U.S. states). Remember that numbers can be used for words. Just think of what the number name sounds like: "1" can be "one" *or* "won"; "8" can be "eight" *or* "ate," etc.

- Think of several ideas first before selecting the license plate that suits you best. Don't just go with your first idea—some of your later ones may be more creative. After you've decided on your message, place your best idea on a piece of construction paper about the size of a license plate. Don't forget to save room for your unique illustration, as most states also allow some unique background designs on their plates. Do all of your printing and drawing in markers or crayon.
- On the back of your plate, write your name and briefly tell what message your license plate intends to send (because others may interpret the message differently).

For Surefire Success

Allow students to work in teams or with partners, if they choose, although each student should still create their own vanity plate. For some kids, the abstract nature of this lesson is initially challenging; discussing their ideas with someone else may help reluctant students to fully take part in the activity.

Classroom Extensions

- Have students who finish early work in small groups to complete Handout 7.1: License Plates of the Rich and Famous (and Others, Too). To take the activity a step further into history and literature, you may wish to have students complete the handout after, or in conjunction with, a biographical study of some of the people cited. Here are some starter ideas for the license plates on the handout:
  o   Abraham Lincoln: 4 SCORE
  o   Rosa Parks: FYT 2 RYD
  o   Lawyer: I SUE U
  o   Computer programmer: I BYTE
  o   Cinderella: SLIP R
  o   Gulliver: BIG N LTL
  o   Boston Tea Party: NOT TAX
  o   Leaning Tower of Pisa: ITALEAN

- Some U.S. states offer a variety of license plate designs from which to choose. For example, some Florida plates highlight Cape Canaveral; Indiana has a plate emblazoned "Put Kids First," printed in a child's scrawl;

and Connecticut's plate features a colorful lighthouse, indicating that state's seacoast location. Have students design a background for a standard license plate for your state or province. Send some of the most creative ideas to your legislators and ask them to consider the designs for adoption.

- Share with your students the amazing artwork "Preamble" by Mike Wilkins (https://americanart.si.edu/artwork/preamble-27722). Created in 1987 and housed at the Smithsonian Museum of American Art, the work is made up entirely of one license plate from each U.S. state, arranged in such a way that it reads as the Preamble to the U.S. Constitution.
- Throughout the year, during any content-based class, extend this activity and have students design license plates for famous musicians, artists, scientists, and historical and literary figures.

School Extension

Sponsor a schoolwide license plate contest devoted to a particular topic. Topics might include Olympic athletes, current events, famous personalities, and fictional characters.

- -

Handout 7.1

License Plates of the Rich and Famous (and Others, Too)

- -

Directions: Write a vanity plate message for one or two choices in each group.

1. **Famous people in history:**

   Thomas Jefferson _____

   Betsy Ross _____

   Abraham Lincoln _____

   Susan B. Anthony _____

   Confucius _____

   Rosa Parks _____

   Juan Ponce de Leon _____

   Frederick Douglass _____

   Indira Gandhi _____

HANDOUT 7.1, continued

2. **Occupations:**

Chef   _____

Lawyer   _____

Artist   _____

Physician   _____

School principal   _____

Computer programmer   _____

3. **Fictional characters and places:**

Bigfoot   _____

E.T.   _____

Cinderella   _____

Land of Oz   _____

Gulliver   _____

Neverland   _____

4. **Historical sites and events:**

Moon Landing   _____

Boston Tea Party   _____

Mount Rushmore   _____

The White House   _____

Leaning Tower of Pisa   _____

Taj Mahal   _____

Pyramids of the Sun
and Moon   _____

Great Wall of China   _____

Activity 8

Celebration Streamers

Celebrations need not mark only momentous occasions. Along the paths traveled in life lie a bounty of notable smaller stops and turns—new accomplishments, heightened understandings, fresh starts, and sheer wonder. Everyone's life is full of moments worth celebrating, yet people often don't take the time to acknowledge the small things that make their days better. This activity provides an opportunity for students to gain an appreciation of these little moments in their lives. As they reflect upon the significance of everyday occurrences, students identify those occasions—some personal and some universal—worth noting and celebrating.

Learning Objectives

Through this activity, students will:
*   identify both small and large aspects of their lives that are worth celebrating,
*   work cooperatively toward a common goal, and
*   explore their own and their classmates' interests and aspirations.

Materials

*   White construction paper
*   Fine line, dark ink markers
*   Device to play soft nature or classical music

85

- Rolls of adding machine tape (precut into 3-foot sections; at least one section per pair of students)
- Pencils, colored pencils, pens, crayons, or markers
- Tape
- Optional:
  - *I'm in Charge of Celebrations* by Byrd Baylor
  - *My Heart Fills With Happiness* by Monique Gray Smith (for younger kids)
  - *The Book of Awesome* by Neil Pasricha (for older kids)

Time

Two 40-minute sessions

Preparation

Prior to the activity, make a list of five things you believe are important to celebrate. Make your list as personal as you like. For example, your list might include seeing the first spring flower bloom, biting into a gooey piece of double chocolate cake, or learning that your daughter or son has been accepted by a college.

Write this list on a sheet of construction paper, using a dark ink marker. Keep your list hidden from students until it is shared later in the lesson.

Activity Steps

1. Set the mood by playing music—something soft, classical, or soothing. Don't speak at first; allow 4–5 minutes for students to take in the softness of the sounds they hear. If students start to fidget, just put a finger to your lips and say, "shhh."
2. Once students are sufficiently relaxed, tell them the activity they are going to do requires thoughtful reflection about the lives they have led, are leading now, or may lead in the future. Ask students to confer with a neighbor or with other students at their table about the meaning of the word *celebration*. Allow 2–3 minutes for students to arrive at a definition of the word with their partners or groups. As students brainstorm, draw two columns on the board, labeled "Definitions" and "Celebrations." Next, have students

(with their partners or groups) name some things that are celebrated. Allow only a few minutes for this brainstorming.

3. Select students to share their ideas orally. Write down the ideas in the columns on the board. This should take only a few minutes.

4. Talk about celebrating "small wonders." Explain to students that they will be expanding their concept of what can be celebrated. If possible, read *My Heart Fills With Happiness* to younger children or selected passages from *The Book of Awesome* to older students (or visit https://1000awesomethings. com for samples from the book). Each book celebrates the small things in life that are often forgotten or bypassed. Discuss with students the meaning of the phrase "stop and smell the roses" and comment briefly on the importance of doing so. Then, share your list of five things you feel are important to celebrate in your own life.

5. A cautionary note: As this lesson evolves, please consider the lives of the students in your class. A certain amount of sensitivity must be exercised in this activity, as some students, depending upon their home lives, may not have much to celebrate—or perhaps their families do not hold celebrations. Thus, you may need to help students see beyond what is traditionally celebrated (e.g., birthdays or holidays) to some of nature's important events (e.g., the first snowfall, the first leaves that turn color in the fall, etc.).

6. Divide students into pairs and challenge partners to brainstorm as many things worth celebrating as they can, following the "small wonders" ideas that you have already discussed. Request a minimum of 15 celebratory ideas from each pair of students. After a few minutes, ask each pair to share a favorite celebration from their lists with the whole class. Although students may be eager to share many ideas, you'll want to limit each pair to one response. This allows everyone a chance to participate.

7. Explain specifically why you like the ideas students shared. Perhaps vocabulary was descriptive, a response was unique, or a thought shed special light on something typically considered mundane. You may also need to urge students to think even more deeply about some potential celebrations no one else may consider.

8. Encourage students to review their lists, elaborate upon those already written, or add more ideas to their lists. Allow approximately 10 minutes for this revision.

9. Instruct pairs to review their lists and mark with an asterisk the 10 they believe to be the most creative and original.

10. Have students transfer their ideas onto adding machine tape and use markers or colored pencils to illustrate and decorate their sections of the tape. Explain that all of the sections will be taped together and displayed for others to read, so their printing and illustrations must be large enough to

be seen from a distance. Allow adequate time for partners to complete their tapes.

11. Once students are finished, have them sit in a circle and share their designated celebrations. As each pair shares, comment on specific elements, such as descriptive words or creative designs, that you especially like about their celebration tapes. Encourage students to make positive comments about their peers' tapes as well.

12. Tape the ends of the sections together to make one or several long strips. Hang the completed strip(s) as part of a display called "Let's Celebrate!" or "We're in the Mood to Celebrate!"

For Surefire Success

- Getting students into an appropriate frame of mind for this activity is critical, and the softness of nature or classical music really helps. Play it during the group work as students brainstorm, write, and complete their celebration ideas.

- An effective way to display the completed tapes is to handle them like crepe paper streamers. Staple or tape them in 12-inch sections and loosely drape them from the ceiling down along the walls. This can be easily accomplished on a suspended ceiling by using a stapler or pushpins. Another idea is to suspend the tapes straight down from the ceiling like ribbons; they might need an anchor of some type, such as a large paper clip, at the bottom, and the printing on the top streamers will need to be large enough for others to read.

Classroom Extensions

- You might wish to use this activity as an introduction to a larger theme or unit of study. Perhaps each month your class can concentrate on one specific thing to celebrate (such as friendship or diversity). Students can write about the topic, create artwork, or do other related activities you assign, which can then be included in your celebrations display.

- If you choose to expand this activity, consider having students select two of their favorite writings or drawings to include in a bound book titled "Our Celebrations." Duplicate the book for students to take home at the end of the year, or post several different celebratory ideas on your class website each time you update it.

School Extension

This activity can easily be expanded to include other classrooms or even the whole school. Think of how wonderful it would be for a visitor to walk into your school and be greeted by a banner announcing, "Let's Celebrate!"—and then look up to see yards of celebration streamers clinging to walls and draped from the ceiling!

Activity 9

Thumbody Like Me

As the school year unfolds, students begin to realize that even though they share many things in common (e.g., grade level, age, interests), they also differ in many ways. To help students consider their own uniqueness and explore it in a creative way, this activity uses each student's one-of-a-kind thumbprint as a central character in a cartoon autobiography. The activity provides class members the opportunity to get to know themselves and each other more fully as they examine how every student is "thumbody" special.

Learning Objectives

Through this activity, students will:
- recognize and appreciate similarities and differences among classmates;
- identify personal strengths, interests, and goals;
- identify significant people in their lives; and
- tell personal stories creatively within an assigned framework.

Materials

- Handout 9.1: Storyboard Template
- Handout 9.2: Thumbody's Story
- Eight index cards

- Pencils
- Ink pads of various colors
- Pens with various colors of ink
- Moist towelettes or baby wipes to clean off thumbprints
- Optional: Laminating material or fixative
- For Classroom Extension: *The Sneetches and Other Stories* by Dr. Seuss

Time

One 30-minute session to introduce the activity; additional at-home or in-class time to create the autobiographies

Activity Steps

1. Ask your students: *What is something unique that you've had since birth, but you probably wouldn't recognize if you saw it?* As students raise their hands to offer responses, invite them to the front of the class to share their answers. Do this until you have 6–8 student volunteers.

2. If none of the students offered "my fingerprints" as an answer to this riddle, tell them that, among the things that make each of them unique, one that often goes unrecognized is the individuality of their fingerprints. Even though no one else on Earth has the exact same set of lines, creases, and crevices on them, most people wouldn't know their fingerprints if they came face-to-face (or face-to-print) with them.

3. Give each student who volunteered an index card. Ask these students to write their names, in pencil, on the side of the index card that has lines. Here's where the fun (and a little mess) occurs: Invite each student volunteer to take their right thumb, press it onto an ink pad, and transfer the print onto the unlined side of the index card. As the students return to their seats, shuffle the index cards.

4. Try to identify thumbprints. Hold up one card and ask: *Whose print is this?* Inevitably, some students will identify the wrong prints as theirs. This proves your assertion that even though they've had these prints since the day they were born, they still can't recognize them. Then say: *Well, that's about to change!*

5. Introduce the activity. Tell your students that they will each have a chance to become more familiar with their own thumbprints: They will use one of their thumbprints to design a cartoon character to introduce themselves

to others. Distribute Handout 9.1: Storyboard Template. Explain that the first frame of the cartoon should read: "Hi! I'm thumbody special. My name is _____, and I'd like to introduce you to my owner." At this point, you may wish to share Handout 9.2: Thumbody's Story with the class so students can see an example of how one student developed a thumbnail autobiography.

6. From there, it's up to your students' imaginations. The additional storyboard frames can show the thumbprint doing the kinds of things students like to do, visiting the places they've gone or would like to go, and envisioning or acting out their plans and dreams.

7. Have students create thumbprint cartoons. Remind students that there are no right or wrong ways to do this activity; they may be very creative in both the content and style of their story. For example:
   - Students could write their story in poetic form, using rhyme or free verse.
   - Students could write their story as a series of riddles (e.g., "I like this summer sport that involves water. Can you guess what sport it is?").
   - Students could move through their lives chronologically, writing about what they were like as young children, who they are now, and who they hope to be as adults.
   - Students could assume an alias and write as if they had spent their lives as someone else—maybe even a space alien!

8. Remind students that they should first compose their story on their practice storyboard, and that they should *only* add the thumbprints on the final version they create. Be sure to have extra paper and plenty of moist towelettes on hand, as there will be some mistakes and smudges along the way. If students want to keep their "Thumbnail Sketches" for posterity, laminate or spray them with fixative soon after they are completed.

9. Once the cartoons are completed, give all students a chance to share their stories with other classmates in small groups, round-robin fashion. Later, invite students to display the autobiographies for everyone to read and enjoy.

For Surefire Success

- Use ink pads of different colors—black, red, purple, and green are fairly easy to find. Then, an "embarrassed" thumbprint can be depicted in red, and one that was hit by a hammer can be black and blue. Combining colors into a single smudge yields some interesting results.

- Have students start by doing a rough draft of the storyboard. Then, for their final copy, have them complete the written part of their story first, We have found that our students have the most fun when adding the thumbprints to their storyboards. However, this should be the *final* step in the process. Why? First, because we want them to complete their stories in writing, which is often less "fun" than the printing. Second, if the thumbprints are placed before the words are added, smudges become inevitable.

Classroom Extension

As a fun follow-up that can also prompt good discussion about the wonder of individual differences, read to your students "The Sneetches" from Dr. Seuss's *The Sneetches and Other Stories* or show the animated version of the story. This metaphorical story goes a long way in getting children to understand that unique or different is not bad—it just is.

Family Extension

If you're looking for an inexpensive and easy holiday gift for students to create for families and other special people, have them make "Thumbody Special" stationery. Their messages might begin with:

- Grandma and Grandpa, you are both thumbody special. Here's why:
- Paul, as a stepdad, you are thumbody special. Here's why:
- Ming-Le, you are "thumb" special sister. Here's why:

Handout 9.1
Storyboard Template

Storyboard Template

HANDOUT 9.1, continued

Storyboard Template

Handout 9.2
Thumbody's Story

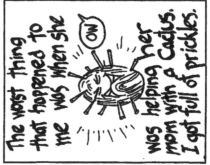

Activity 10

Filling Our Own Shoes

Goals are meant to inspire—to urge people to pursue what matters the most to them. Thinking of ways to achieve goals, though, is more challenging, yet ultimately, quite rewarding. This activity stretches students' thinking as they explore the specific characteristics required to turn their dreams into realities. Use it as an enrichment activity for a study of leaders and leadership. In this activity, students will work in teams to create and "fill" shoes with the traits and skills that lead to success. The shoes your students will craft are larger than life—as are the leaders about whom students are thinking.

Learning Objectives

Through this activity, students will:
- think critically about traits of leadership,
- identify qualities of successful people,
- consider how to turn dreams into realities,
- think and work cooperatively, and
- reflect on attributes that may be viewed as inherent versus those that are developed.

Materials

- Handout 10.1: One Filled Shoe
- Large sheets of white butcher paper (approximately 3' x 5'; one sheet per team of three students)
- Scissors
- Markers or pens

- Oher decorative art materials, such as paints, shoelaces, ribbons, glitter
- For Classroom Extension: *50 American Heroes Every Kid Should Meet* by Dennis Denenberg and Lorraine Roscoe

Time

Two or three 40-minute sessions

Preparation

Write or display the following questions on the board:
- What does it mean to "follow in someone else's footsteps"?
- What does it mean when someone says, "Those are hard shoes to fill"?

Activity Steps

1. Ask students to ponder the two questions on the board. Chart responses to each of the questions and encourage specific examples of someone they know who followed in someone else's footsteps filled shoes that were hard to fill. Students can name either someone they know personally or a historical or famous person in other content areas. Depending upon your room arrangement, you might invite them to discuss the possible meanings of these statements with one or two other students, or with the other students at their table. Allow 10 minutes for the discussion.

2. Discuss the ideas as a class. Once students have cited several examples, deepen the discussion by asking for the following elaborations:
   - What kinds of characteristics are generally associated with people we admire? What about with people we consider to be successful and effective leaders?
   - In what ways might these people have achieved their status or goals? What personal qualities would help them to be recognized by others as leaders?
   - Can you provide a couple of examples of people who might have been considered leaders but actually did more harm than good? (*Note.* This question requires a certain level of maturity from students.)

It isn't necessary to get into an in-depth discussion about the definitions of leadership or success. Your purpose is to have students generate a list of personal characteristics (e.g., pride in one's work, passion for one's mission) and other attributes (e.g., a willingness to work hard, being able to bounce back after a setback or defeat) that would help leaders to achieve their goals.

3. Now, return to the original questions about having big shoes to fill and following in someone else's footsteps. Ask students if the same characteristics and attributes would apply to individuals they perceive to be leaders. You might end this discussion by saying: *Well, it seems that if someone has big shoes to fill, they would need to have a lot of the same qualities of our most well-known leaders. Would you agree?*

4. Personalize the ideas in small groups. Place students into teams of three. Challenge them to think of ways that they can "fill their own shoes," no matter what particular goal they are trying to reach. In other words, what personal traits, characteristics, or behaviors might they need to accomplish goals that are important to them? Display or distribute the example provided in Handout 10.1: One Filled Shoe. If your class needs more specifics, you might wish to designate a certain number of personality characteristics (e.g., honesty) and a specific number of strategies (e.g., taking risks or practicing a sport or instrument for longer than expected) to include on their shoes.

5. This step of the activity requires a good deal of guidance because many students will be content with their initial ideas. Encourage students to think deeply about the traits that lead to success, as well as the challenges leaders may have encountered in their lives. If it helps to pick a specific person familiar to all (or most) of the students to personalize the necessary leadership attributes, feel free to do so.

6. When the teams complete this step, ask them to mark with an asterisk the ideas that represent their best thinking about the characteristics of effective leaders. These are the ideas that they will include on their shoe.

7. Have groups plan the design for their shoes. Stress that they should be as creative as possible, and that the design of the shoe should reflect the personalities of all of the group's members. For example, someone might suggest that a hiking boot is a good design to use because leaders often have to walk through tough terrain in order to achieve their goals; another student might suggest a slipper because many leaders have to use a quieter, less forceful method to convince people who don't like their ideas. Encourage students to think about how the shoe design is symbolic of the skills and attributes that effective leaders need.

8. After approving the shoes' designs, distribute butcher paper and other art supplies, and give the go-ahead for students to construct their shoes.
9. Provide an opportunity for the teams to share their work and ideas with others. Then, display the shoes. They might be suspended from the ceiling of your classroom or "marching" along the walls of the school hallways.

For Surefire Success

Introduce this lesson by having a student interview you as you role-play as a leader you admire or think your students would find interesting. If you choose to do this, prepare a series of questions for the student interviewer to use. These questions should focus on your journey toward greatness.

Classroom Extension

You can easily adapt this activity to focus on specific people (perhaps as a conclusion for a unit on biographies) or within a specific area (e.g., "scientists"). If you choose to use this lesson as a connection to a specific topic or unit of study, you might direct each group to focus on one specific individual. For example, during a study of U.S. presidents, each group could select a little-known president and include personality characteristics, barriers overcome, and goals achieved. A great resource for this extension activity is *50 American Heroes Every Kid Should Meet*, which includes a diverse collection of historical and current leaders from politics, medicine, the arts, and sports.

Handout 10.1
One Filled Shoe

Here is a shoe inspired by a team of fourth-grade students.

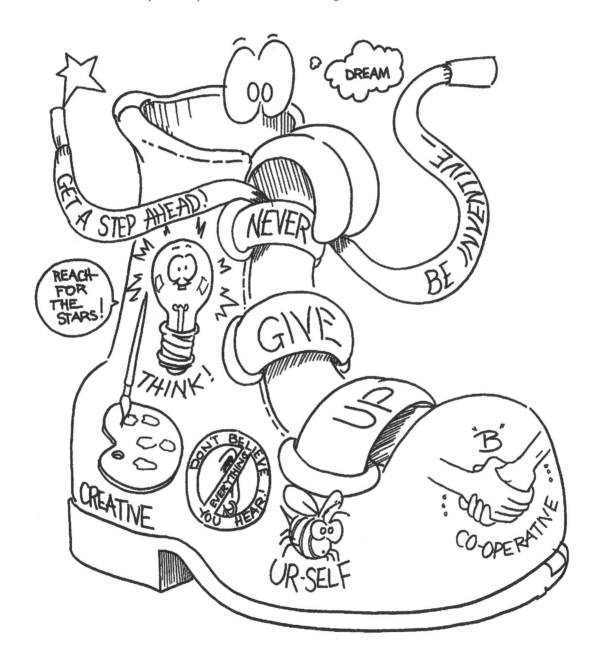

Activity 11

Good Things Come to Those Who Wait

A great challenge of teaching is helping students recognize the components that are essential to personal success. In a culture of instant gratification, it's difficult for students to view time, effort, and patience as essential "ingredients" in reaching goals that are complex or multifaceted. In this activity, students will examine their personal goals in an effort to help them better understand that life's richest experiences depend upon the wise use of those essential elements of success: the aforementioned time, effort, and patience.

Learning Objectives

Through this activity, students will:
- identify activities worthy of consideration;
- work and think cooperatively;
- identify personal values, interests, and goals;
- evaluate ideas and offer constructive, positive feedback;
- understand that reaching long-term goals takes both effort and time; and
- recognize that waiting can yield positive results.

Materials

- Handout 11.1: Patience Pays
- Chart paper or newsprint (two sheets per group of 3–4 students)
- Pencils, colored pencils, pens, crayons, markers, or paints
- Other decorative art materials for illustrating the lists
- Optional: *The Little Engine That Could* by Watty Piper

- For Variation: Materials for making books (see Handout 3.1: Four Ways to Make a Book)

Time

One or two 40-minute sessions, depending upon the depth of the class discussions

Activity Steps

1. Begin by writing on the board: *Good things come to those who wait*. Ask students to explain what they think the statement means. Expand their thinking by encouraging them to consider a variety of perspectives. What might that statement mean to an NBA basketball star, a scientist, a musician, or a parent? List students' ideas on the board. Limit this discussion to 5–7 minutes.

2. After students share their thoughts, raise the idea that waiting is not necessarily a passive activity in which nothing happens. Rather, it can be a meaningful period in which ideas take shape, talents develop, or (in the case of flowers) spring bulbs blossom!

3. Divide the class into groups of 3–4 students and give each group a sheet of chart paper or newsprint. Explain that they will have 10 minutes to brainstorm a list of things that take time to accomplish. You might offer a few suggestions to get them started (e.g., learning to play a musical instrument, learning to read, becoming a good swimmer, or mastering a video game).

4. After 10 minutes, display or distribute Handout 11.1: Patience Pays, discussing just a few items from this list. Encourage students to use these examples as a springboard for adding to and enhancing their own ideas. To get your students thinking beyond obvious skill-based activities, like learning to swim or read, share some of the more abstract ideas from the handout (e.g., becoming wise, learning to be a good friend). Students should see that these more conceptual goals are also likely to take time, effort, and patience to achieve.

5. Challenge groups to return to their lists for 10 more minutes to add additional ideas. If students get stuck, remind them that they should keep going as some new ideas will eventually surface. Once the group discussions end, ask students to react positively to others' ideas. For example, what item on

each list is the most creative? What is most unique or unusual? What item would benefit others, not just themselves (e.g., making a new friend)?

6. Talk about reaching goals. Ask students to consider which items on their lists are likely to be accomplished with the least amount of time and effort (short-term goals) and which ones are likely to take longer, more intense attention (long-term goals). Have a class discussion about goals and the process used to reach them. End this discussion by helping students identify those meaningful aspects in their lives (e.g., peace, friendship) that can't be purchased but do require time and patience to cultivate. You may also like to have students explore the difficulty of waiting, which requires patience and trust.

7. Give each group clean sheets of chart paper or newsprint. Tell groups to select from their brainstormed ideas 15 items that they consider most important. Explain that they should list these and add illustrations to make their chart visually appealing, as noted on the Handout 11.1: Patience Pays.

8. Display the lists. Arrange the lists on a wall or bulletin board under the title "Good Things Come to Those Who Wait."

For Surefire Success

- Sit with each brainstorming group and offer a specific idea, especially one that involves an abstract concept, to encourage students to expand their thinking.
- Challenge students to think beyond the obvious. Coax them away from (or, at least, minimize) materialistic goals like "becoming rich" or "having the most expensive car in the neighborhood." Depending upon your students, you might even consider limiting the number of items or activities that involve money.
- If you want to introduce this lesson with a time-tested classic, read *The Little Engine That Could* to your students. This children's book carries a message that is as important today as when it was written in 1930: Perseverance and kindness pay off in the long run.

Variation

Compile the lists into a book format. Provide a copy to the school library, give out copies to families during an open house, or leave copies in public places, such as the office waiting area, the local library, or a doctor's waiting room.

Handout 11.1
Patience Pays

A group of sixth graders developed this list.

baking a
cake

These things take time:

learning to be a good friend
watching a sunset
listening to a child's story
building a home
learning a different language
becoming wise
growing into an adult
reading a mystery book
earning money
knowing oneself

writing a
symphony

turning coal into
diamonds

making the planet a
healthier place

pretending

Activity 12

Possible Dreams

The term *daydreaming* is often construed negatively, as critics assume that daydreamers are wasting their time pursuing useless or impossible things. We couldn't disagree more, as we believe that daydreamers are the architects of the possible—creative wanderers whose thoughts run toward all manner of accomplishments that are anything but frivolous. In this activity, students will accept that daydreams might become reality, thanks to an adventurer who, from age 15, daydreamed his way to unforgettable life experiences. As your students learn about the real-world experiences of John Goddard, they may begin to see just how important it is to make and follow through on goals and dreams that others might see as fantastical. From there, students begin their own adventures in charting life goals. As your students proceed through this activity, you will gain keen insights into the hopes and goals they harbor.

Learning Objectives

Through this activity, students will:
- recognize the importance of setting goals,
- contemplate and set goals for themselves, and
- think critically and creatively about life events to which they aspire.

Materials

- Handout 12.1: John Goddard's Daydreams and Goals
- Handout 12.2: One Student's Possible Dreams

109

- Handout 12.3: My Personal Goals and Possible Dreams
- Colored pencils, crayons, or markers
- Video: "John Goddard: The List and Life of an Adventurer" (https://www.youtube.com/watch?v=92XYY-rCg8I)
- Optional: John Goddard costume (faded and patched blue jeans, flannel shirt, hiking boots, and bandana)

Time

One 45-minute session to introduce the activity; additional at-home or in-school time to write goals

Background

John Goddard was a man of many accomplishments. In his lifetime, he scaled Mts. Rainier and Fuji as well as the Matterhorn. He retraced Marco Polo's route through the Orient and swam in Africa's Lake Victoria. He landed on and took off from an aircraft carrier and piloted highspeed planes, including an F-111. He earned the rank of Eagle Scout and learned to play both the flute and violin. Obviously, Goddard was big on adventure—and on goal-setting.

One of Goddard's greatest accomplishments, and the one about which he wrote his book *Kayaks Down the Nile*, was the time he and two friends kayaked the entire length of the Nile River (4,145 miles); they were the first persons to do so in kayaks. This 9-month voyage was filled with adventures with the flora, fauna, and people of Africa.

Activity Steps

1. This activity gives you an excuse to dress up as someone else and impress your students with your versatility. In costume as John Goddard (frayed blue jeans, flannel shirt, hiking boots, bandana, etc.), introduce yourself by name, and ask if your students know who you are. (Trust us, they won't!)
2. Tell students about Goddard's experience traveling the Nile. Then, in character, begin to detail some of Goddard's accomplishments, sharing the video of his life and adventures.
3. Once you have finished detailing your kayaking trip, tell students that this adventure was neither your first nor your last one. In fact, explain that you

took this challenging trip because when you were 15 years old you made a list of 127 daydreams and goals you wanted to accomplish in your lifetime. Add that, over the years, your list grew to include 227 dreams and goals.

4. Display or distribute Handout 12.1: John Goddard's Daydreams and Goals, which highlights some of what Goddard accomplished over a span of more than 55 years. Invite comments and questions on any goals that seem particularly interesting, such as becoming skilled is using a boomerang or learning to speak Arabic. Tell students that Goddard, who died in 2012 (perhaps one of your students can research his obituary), realized more than three-quarters of the goals and dreams he set for himself. Among the dreams he did not get fulfill was visiting the moon (but he did get to build a telescope) and milking a poisonous snake. For a complete list of Goddard's 127 goals he wrote at age 15, visit https://johngoddard.info/life_list.htm.

5. After discussing some adventurous dreams and goals that your own students might pursue, distribute Handout 12.2: One Student's Possible Dreams, which shows one seventh-grade student's goals and daydreams. Briefly discuss the list with students; suggest that they use it to spark their own ideas about feats both large and small that they wish to accomplish in their lives.

6. Distribute Handout 12.3: My Personal Goals and Possible Dreams. Challenge students to devise their own individual lists of lifetime possibilities, using both Goddard's list and Handout 12.2 as "idea instigators." What places do they hope to visit? Whom would they like to meet? What would they like to learn to do? What would they like to explore, study, read, eat, or experience? The items and categories are limited only by students' imaginations. Tell students to organize, format, and decorate their lists in whatever way they wish.

7. As students prepare their lists, ask them to think beyond meeting people who have only recently become famous. Otherwise, you'll end up getting the athlete or performer *du jour* on each student's wish list. Perhaps they can think of people in categories other than sports or media; give some possible examples from history or current events to help them get started.

8. Tell students they will have one week to compile their lists. During this time, they should spend at least 15 minutes each day thinking about and writing down ideas. (Whether this is done during class time or at home is up to you.)

9. When a week has passed, have students share their completed lists in groups of 3–4. Finally, have each student ask a witness to sign the list. Tell students to take these lists home and keep them someplace safe. If they want to emulate how you introduced this activity—by dressing up in some John Goddard-like garb—as they share their lists, why not?

For Surefire Success

- By taking on the character of John Goddard yourself, you will greatly enhance this activity. Kids love it when their teachers dress up as some-one else—it lets them see both your playfulness and your ingenuity. If you choose to dress up, make sure to stay in character and take your role seriously. Your students really will see you as the person you're pretending to be only if you assume this persona.
- Make up your own list and share it (in total or part) with your students. This shows them that even though adults have "grown up," they continue to have goals, too.

Variation

At the beginning of the school year, term, or vacation break, have students write letters to themselves detailing their goals for the next several months. Collect the letters and, several weeks or months later, return them to students for their reactions and reflections. One teacher we know kept them and mailed them to the students when they graduated from high school.

Handout 12.1
John Goddard's Daydreams and Goals

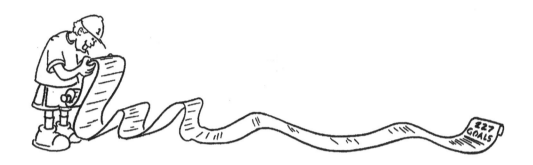

In his lifetime, John Goddard set 227 goals for himself, accomplishing more than three-quarters of them before he died. Here are some of the goals Goddard reached.

> Explore the Nile, Amazon, Congo, and Rio Coco Rivers.
> Learn French, Spanish, and Arabic.
> Climb Mts. Kilimanjaro, Ararat, Rainier, Fuji, and Vesuvius.
> Pilot a plane, motorcycle, tractor, and canoe.
> Swim in Lakes Victoria, Superior, Tanganyika, Titicaca, and Nicaragua.
> Become skilled in using a surfboard, football, basketball, lariat, and boomerang.
> Explore the Great Barrier Reef, Red Sea, Fiji Islands, Okefenokee Swamp, and Everglades.
> Read the works of Dickens, Emerson, Hemingway, Longfellow, Plato, Poe, Shakespeare, Tolstoy, and Twain.
> Carry out careers in medicine and exploration.
> Become familiar with the music of Bach, Beethoven, Debussy, Ravel, Rachmaninoff, Rimsky-Korsakov, Tchaikovsky, and Verdi.
> Learn fencing and jujitsu.
> Build a telescope.
> Write a book and an article for *National Geographic.*
> Circumnavigate the globe (he did—four times).
> Run a mile in 5 minutes.
> Marry and have children (he has five).

Handout 12.2
One Student's Possible Dreams

Here is a goal list created by a seventh-grade student.

Places to explore:

1. The North Pole
2. Every U.S. state
3. An Indian reservation in Arizona
4. The Great Barrier Reef
5. The attic of a haunted house
6. A castle in England
7. The Oval Office

People to meet:

1. A past U.S. president
2. My uncle who lives in Israel
3. The Chicago Bulls—all of them
4. An animator from PIXAR
5. The owner of a movie studio

Things to learn to do:

1. Scuba dive
2. Create a cartoon character
3. Surf
4. Invent a video game
5. Drive a car with a stick shift
6. Produce a short movie using special effects

Physical accomplishments:

1. Run a mile in less than 4 minutes
2. Build a treehouse by myself
3. Walk through every country in Asia
4. Eat nothing but candy for one week
5. Outrun a dangerous animal that's chasing me

Other goals:

1. Appear in a horror movie
2. Have three kids and two dogs
3. Invent something that will stop pollution
4. Work in a homeless shelter
5. Whitewater raft
6. Spit off the top of the Eiffel Tower
7. Meet Steven Spielberg
8. Own a red sports car
9. Connect the moon and the Earth with paper clips

Handout 12.3
My Personal Goals and Possible Dreams

Directions: Use this sheet to record your own dreams and goals.

Signed on this date, _____, I hope to accomplish these goals in my lifetime. I understand I can add to this list at any time.

_____
Signature

_____
Witness

Part II
Activities for Growing With the World

Activity 13

365 Days of Helping Others

Some children and many adults make New Year's resolutions. Generally, they are personal in nature—to exercise more, to eat healthier, etc.—and indicate one's desire for a fresh start or a reboot of past good habits. Using resolutions, students can focus on ways to make positive changes at home, with friends, at school, and in their community. And what better medium for recording resolutions than a calendar that gives the person using it something different and fresh to look at and ponder every 30 days or so?

This activity calls on students to consider ways to help other people 365 days a year. We suggest introducing this project right after Thanksgiving, when students are already in a holiday mood, counting the days until their winter break. An added benefit of this group project is that the calendar makes a perfect holiday gift.

Learning Objectives

Through this activity, students will:
- define realistic goals,
- work cooperatively toward a broad goal,
- work creatively within a standard format,
- consider and set personal commitments, and
- plan and carry out a project over several days.

Materials

- Handout 13.1: Potential Themes for Helping Month by Month
- Handout 13.2: Calendar Template

- A sampling of calendars for the coming year and from current or past years
- Crayons or markers
- Pencils and fine line markers
- Binding machine or paper punch, and yarn or stapler

Time

One 30-minute session to introduce the activity; additional at-home and in-school time to complete it

Activity Steps

1. Write or display these sentences on the board:
   - I'll lose 15 pounds.
   - I'll exercise more.
   - I'll make one new friend.
   - I'll try to be more patient.

   Ask students if they've ever heard anyone say any of these statements. Then ask: *What do these statements have in common? Is there a particular time of year when you usually hear statements like these from grownups?*
2. Inevitably, several students will mention New Year's resolutions. Ask if anyone's family makes resolutions collectively or if family members do so individually; invite students to give a few examples of resolutions they've heard. Next, ask students if any of them has ever made a New Year's resolution, such as "I'll improve my grades," "I won't fight with my sister," or "I'll do my homework."
3. Then proceed with a discussion: How long do these resolutions usually last before they are broken or forgotten? For example, how long does it take before the dieter nibbles at a piece of chocolate cake, or a big brother yells at his sister for messing with his Xbox? Your students will get the hint: Usually, resolutions last only as long as one's willpower can tolerate the change.
4. Tell students: *Today we're going to plan for the future—your future—by making some resolutions that might really last all year. We'll base our resolutions on promises that are worth keeping, and we'll put them into a calendar, so you'll have daily reminders of your good intentions.*

5. Divide students into 12 working groups. Show students Handout 13.1: Potential Themes for Helping Month by Month, or, if you wish, decide with students on 12 topics of interest to them. Explain that each group will be responsible for creating a calendar page for one month. Assign the months' topics randomly to groups.

6. Give each group several sheets of paper and Handout 13.2: Calendar Template. Make the sample calendars you have collected available to all groups so students can get ideas for illustrations or designs.

7. Have each group create the calendar for its month. This is a lot of work, and it will take several small-group meetings to accomplish. One suggested way to divide the work is as follows:

   - **Task A: Illustrate.** Have several students design an illustration that corresponds to the month's theme.

   - **Task B: Note days, dates, and holidays.** On Handout 13.2, label the month and days for the coming new year, using the small boxes within each box to place the numerical dates. Place all national and state holidays in the appropriate spaces on the calendar. (*Note.* It's helpful to have a master calendar available so you have the exact dates for "floating" holidays, like Thanksgiving or President's Day.) For best results, tell students to print lightly with a pencil first, check their spelling, and then print over the pencil with a black, fine line marker. Spaces to write are small, so they must keep the messages brief. If everyone has access to a digital tool, such as a computer, laptop, or tablet, these can be used as well.

   - **Task C: Create resolutions.** For the remaining calendar days (that are not holidays), devise resolutions that fit the month's theme, such as "Invite a new kid to sleep over" or "Recycle your plastic." Suggest that for some days of each month, groups might include illustrations instead of words. For example, a picture of two kids shaking hands (representing making friends or making mutual decisions) could occupy a day or two for a given month.

8. Groups working on different months may generate similar ideas for some days. Assure students that this is okay. After all, some good resolutions are worth repeating!

9. Create a cover for the calendar. Appoint or have students appoint a committee of 3–4 students to design a cover for the calendar that represents many of the ideas reflected on its pages. Perhaps some of your class's artists will volunteer for this task.

10. Assemble the calendar. Your finished product will be a monthly calendar, 11" x 17", with a spiral bind in the middle. If you do not have access to a

binding machine, connect the pages with yarn or staple them.

11. Be sure to keep a set of unbound originals for duplicating more copies of the calendar.

12. Distribute calendars. Distribute copies of the calendar for students' personal use or for presenting as holiday gifts to friends and family.

For Surefire Success

- Have students brainstorm multiple ideas for their calendar pages before completing their final copy.
- Encourage students to balance serious and humorous resolutions. Of course, do not allow inappropriate topics.
- Before completing a final copy, have an editor (perhaps you or a parent volunteer) review spelling, grammar, and appropriateness of content.

School Extensions

- Use the calendars as a fundraising item for a school or community project.
- Provide the principal, superintendent, school board members, and the local community's governing body with copies. This is great PR!

Handout 13.1
Potential Themes for Helping Month by Month

JANUARY
Keeping healthy so we can help others

FEBRUARY
Increasing our understanding of people who differ from us

MARCH
Improving our relationships with friends or siblings

APRIL
Cleaning up or improving the environment

MAY
Bringing small rays of sunshine into people's lives

JUNE
Improving relationships with family members

JULY
Celebrating our own backgrounds and our nation's heritage

AUGUST
Keeping cool when tempers get hot

SEPTEMBER
Setting and maintaining positive attitudes toward school

OCTOBER
Making the world a less scary place

NOVEMBER
Showing thanks to people we care about

DECEMBER
Being generous to others

123

Handout 13.2
Calendar Template

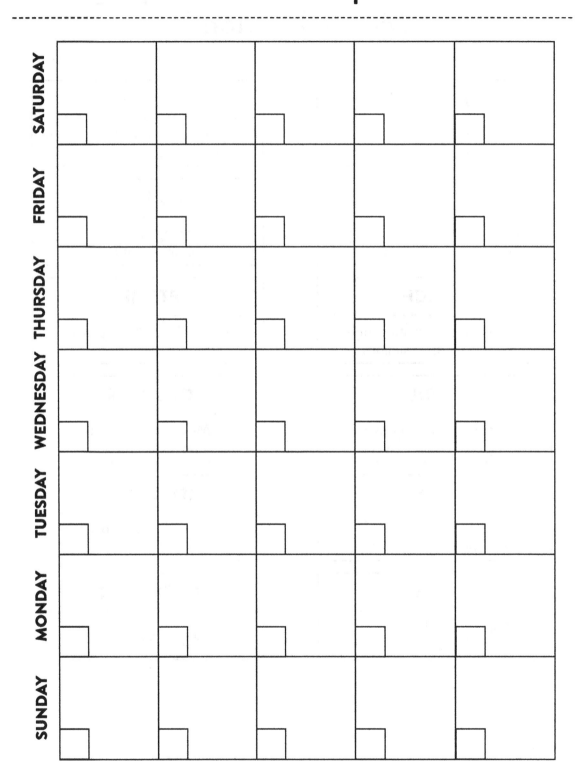

Activity 14

Heart to Heart

Many students are naturally inclined to want to aid others whom they believe need help or hope. Too seldom, though, do teachers actually *encourage* kids to act on their caring by reaching out. This activity enables students to connect, via written communication, to individuals they have never met. By offering messages of hope and optimism to strangers, students may come to recognize empathy as an important feeling to develop and nurture. Additionally, the art of writing letters—something seldom, if ever, done by young children—takes on a new and relevant meaning.

Learning Objectives

Through this activity, students will:
- recognize the needs of others,
- empathize with people whom they do not know personally,
- recognize and act on their own capacity to support other people,
- work and think cooperatively, and
- compose and write letters of support and encouragement.

Materials

- Handout 14.1: Heartfelt Communication
- Several newspaper sections from a recent local or regional newspaper (per pair of students)
- Large sheet of red construction paper (per pair of students)
- Scissors
- Paste or glue
- Envelope and stamp (per pair of students)
- Optional: *Miss Rumphius* by Barbara Cooney
- For Classroom and School Extension: map, pushpins, and small hearts to pin to the map

Time

One or two 40-minute sessions

Preparation

Select a news story (and photo, if available) that describes people doing something positive for others in the local or regional community. If you can find examples of youth helping others, this would benefit the lesson. Also select one additional news story that will easily elicit a feeling of concern or empathy and a desire to offer support and hope.

Activity Steps

1. Start by sharing the first news article or picture you selected—your "good news." Invite students to comment on what the person or activity has done to make the world a kinder or better place, even if it is a small step for the better.

2. Optional: If you have a copy of *Miss Rumphius*, read this story to your students and discuss the three lessons Miss Rumphius's grandfather taught her. Ask students to comment on the last lesson, described as the most important one by her grandfather: to make the world a more beautiful

place. If you can't locate a copy in your school or local library, there are several read-aloud versions available on YouTube.

3. Discuss ideas for making a better world. Ask students: *What are some ways adults and children can make the world a kinder or more beautiful place?* List students' ideas on the board in two categories, "Adults" and "Children/Young People." Remind students that these good deeds do not have to be huge tasks affecting thousands of people (although, they might); even something positive that affects only one or a few persons is still an important contribution.

4. After students have generated sizable lists, review their ideas and discuss what makes particular entries meaningful—to an individual, a group, the planet's health, etc. Explain to students that even the smallest kindness, such as shoveling an elderly neighbor's snow for free, can make a person's day better than it might have been.

5. Divide the class into pairs and assign one or two newspaper sections to each pair of kids. Explain that their task is to locate a picture or an article that interests them, one that could warrant a positive response, such as a compliment or note of support to the person(s) about whom the story is written.

6. Once students have located several stories about providing kindness or help, ask students to summarize to the class the story they selected. At this point, ask what they might want to say to the person or people whose good deeds were highlighted in the news articles. Encourage specific suggestions, such as "I'd like to thank them for doing a litter cleanup at the beach because it's such a beautiful place and needs to stay that way." Provide two specific examples to students, using the articles you have already shown as well as another one you selected in your preparation. Students may select any type of news, as long as they can think of a compliment or some words of hope and support in response to it. Remind students that they need to be very specific in their comments.

7. Ask your students if they ever received a letter or birthday card in the mail. If so, how did it make them feel when they got the envelope? Most are likely to say "excited" or "happy," as in this era of electronic communications, physical letters and cards are few and far between. Explain that even adults feel this same sense of excitement when they open their mailbox and find something other than a bill or advertisement. The class is going to "make someone's day" by writing and sending actual letters thanking them for their efforts on behalf of others. Students should cut out their selected articles or pictures and then draft a letter to the individuals involved. Their letters should offer a compliment, words of encouragement, or some spe-

cific support to the people highlighted in the news article. Offer a concrete example by sharing Handout 14.1: Heartfelt Communication.

8. As groups work, circulate among students and offer suggestions and help as needed. Sometimes they will need concrete ideas to help them get started. They might also need to be guided from using a general statement (e.g., "We like what you did.") to something more specific (e.g., "Providing meals to newly arrived immigrants must have made them feel very welcomed."). Give groups clean sheets of writing paper on which to write the final versions of their letters.

9. Create copies of the letters and have students mail the originals to the individuals involved in care of the newspaper that ran the stories.

10. After partners have completed their letters, have them create heart displays. Give them red construction paper and have them cut out a large heart and fold it in half. On one half of the heart they will glue their news article; on the other half, their photocopied letter.

11. Invite pairs to share their articles and accompanying letters. A class discussion on the meaning of empathy and caring for others should naturally evolve. Prompt students to relate this activity to the challenge of bettering the world by asking:
    - How does a simple message of hope and caring to people we don't even know help to make the world a more beautiful place?
    - Why is it important to reach out to people in this way?
    - How does this simple act help to plant seeds of kindness?

    Incorporate the notion that each person can easily take relatively cost-free steps to make the world a kinder or more beautiful place.

12. Display the hearts for others to read. Some suggested bulletin board or hallway headings are "Heartfelt Messages," "Communicating With a Heart," or "Caring Communications."

For Surefire Success

This activity can easily generate much enthusiasm, especially if you show students your own excitement about the possibilities. Share a letter you have written to encourage someone or to offer a message of hope. If you don't have one to share, describe why the news articles you selected inspired you.

Classroom Extensions

- Challenge students to independently locate another news article that elicits the same feelings as those in this activity. Give students 3–5 days to locate the news and write an accompanying letter to the individuals involved. Suggest that students mail these letters, too. It might take some effort to locate addresses, but remind students that things worth doing are not always easy. Encourage students to consult the local newspaper or library for help, check with the agencies or organizations associated with the story, or look for addresses online.
- Keep your bulletin board display up for a full term or year and use it to post copies of letters mailed by your students to others. Encourage students to continue to write and post letters throughout the year. If students receive return mail, display this correspondence as well. You might even wish to include a map and use pushpins to mark the locations where correspondents live, reminding your students how many people have been affected by their caring.
- Create good news of your own. Contact the media and let them know about your project and the results. They might publish a story about your class!

School Extension

Encourage other classes (or even the whole school) to join your class in meeting the challenge of making the world a kinder or more beautiful place. You might even expand your efforts beyond the local or regional area and locate individuals or groups that could use a heartfelt thank you from kids they've never met. Then, keep track of the letters mailed from and to students and post a map outside the school office on which students pin a heart for each letter sent.

Handout 14.1
Heartfelt Communication

Here is a letter written by two sixth-grade students.

May 1, 2020

Dear Dr. Margaret Deland,

We read an article about you in the *Daily Times* on January 4, 2020, about how you perform cleft palate surgery on children for free when their families do not have enough money or insurance to cover the cost. We were extremely impressed and inspired by your kindness and generosity. The world needs more doctors like you who don't work just for the money but for the joy of serving others. A surge of happiness rushed through us both when we read about your work. Even though you didn't do the surgery for either of us, we can't thank you enough. We're so glad that kids like Sigi, who was highlighted in the newspaper story, can now lead a more normal life. Keep up the great work and don't ever change your truly magnificent principles!

Sincerely,
Paulo and Melanie

Activity 15

The Footpath of Peace

With violence and anger spewing daily from so many media outlets, it is sometimes hard to believe that the world is, indeed, filled with more good people than bad, more beauty than bigotry. This activity helps students to recognize that there is much that is positive about their world and, equally important, that each person can be an agent of change to make the world even better than it already is. In this activity, students learn that peaceful change begins with small steps. By hearing about ways that people have chosen to act kindly toward others, students see the benefits of their own kind behaviors and will be encouraged to add their own steps on the Footpath of Peace.

Learning Objectives

Through this activity, students will:
- recognize that people are interdependent,
- identify kindnesses they have done for others,
- identify kindnesses that others have done for them, and
- write personal accounts about living peacefully and interdependently.

Materials

- Handout 15.1: Footprints of Peace
- Light-colored construction paper (one sheet per student)
- Pens, crayons, or markers
- Optional: *Random Acts of Kindness* by the editors of Conari Press or *The Invisible Boy* by Trudy Ludwig

Time

One 55-minute session

Activity Steps

1. As students enter your class, have the following quote visible for all to see: "We may have all come on different ships, but we're in the same boat now."—Dr. Martin Luther King, Jr.

2. Ask for several interpretations of this quote and gauge how much students know about King's life and legacy. If necessary, provide a brief overview of King's life, emphasizing his lifelong desire to see change occur peacefully and to have all people be accepted as worthwhile individuals.

3. Next, display these additional quotes:
   - "It's fearful to know we're connected to everything in the universe, because then we're responsible."—Glenda Taylor
   - "The purpose of life is a life with a purpose."—Robert Byrne
   - "If there is any kindness I can show, or any good thing I can do to any fellow being, let me do it now, as I shall not pass this way again."—William Penn
   - "See the squirrel? That's your brother. See the tree? We are related. This is your family; these are all your family."—Brooke Medicine Eagle
   - "Whenever you are to do a thing, ask yourself how you would act were all the world looking at you, and act accordingly."—Thomas Jefferson
   - "I think the best way to find happiness is to stop looking so hard."—Kermit the Frog

4. Ask for volunteers to state what common ideas or sentiments are being expressed in all of these quotations. You might find it advantageous to have students discuss ideas in small groups or with partners before sharing

with the whole class. It shouldn't take long before one of your students says something like, "All of these quotes express the feeling that people have to help each other out," or "Even though each person is an individual, we still have to live together and help each other."

5. Talk about acts of kindness. Remind students that the kind acts people do are not necessarily the things that appear in the news or online. In fact, some of the most important and memorable kind acts can be noted in small, everyday actions. As proof, discuss these questions with your students:

    • Even though it's a pain, have you or has someone in your family ever returned a shopping cart to its appointed space instead of just leaving it out in the parking lot? Why did you do this? Whom did it help?

    • Even if you didn't drop it yourself, did you ever pick up a piece of trash in the school hallway and throw it away properly? Why did you do this? Whom did it help?

    • Did you ever send a letter to a teacher or camp counselor or relative to say that the person made a difference in your life? Why did you do this? Whom did it help?

    • Did you ever ask an older person to tell you a story about her life—memories of school, how she met her spouse, a favorite song? Why did you do this? Whom did it help?

6. Tell students that each of the actions they've discussed is a small step toward making the world a kinder place. Return to each of the quotes shared earlier that express the belief that even little things can improve people's understanding of one another. Explain that students will now share some of their own actions that follow in the footsteps of these others.

7. Optional: At this point, you may wish to read *Random Acts of Kindness*, *The Invisible Boy*, or any other of your favorite readings about how small acts of kindness can be important in the lives of others.

8. Create footprints for a footpath. Here's where the fun begins. Invite your students to take off one of their shoes and trace the shoe onto a piece of construction paper. On this "footprint," they should write one act of kindness that they have done for someone else or that someone else has done for them. Display or distribute Handout 15.1: Footprints of Peace and discuss some of the ideas these fourth-grade students included in their footprints.

9. Encourage students to decorate the footprints as wildly as they like, as long as the writing can be read easily. When the footprints are complete, display them as a footpath along the wall of a school hallway. Point out that, as students walk by this wall, they will see that everyone is helping to make the world a kinder place one small step at a time.

For Surefire Success

To ensure an equal number of left and right footprints to display, have students count off (one-two or right-left) before they trace their feet.

Classroom Extension

International Random Acts of Kindness Day is celebrated every February 17, as people from across the globe share stories of small acts that made a big difference. Celebrate this day by completing the Footpath of Peace as a schoolwide venture.

Handout 15.1
Footprints of Peace

Here are some students' footprints of peace.

I was walking down the hall in school and I saw this person getting picked on, so I stopped the other person from picking on him.

I ate my mother's stew dinner, even though it was not very good, because I knew she worked hard cooking it.

In third grade I had a good teacher and I already knew him, so I invited him to my house for dinner. Not to be a suck up, but to be a good person. I felt good I did it.

At Christmas-time, my older sister told my little sister that there was no Santa Claus, so I gave her a gift every day until Christmas and said it was from Santa. This really made my little sister feel good!

One day I gave the guy who picks up our trash a Snickers bar. Then the next time he came around he gave me a Milky Way.

I once lived by a lonely man and a lonely dog. Instead of going out to play, I would always go over and talk to the man and play with the dog.

135

"I've learned goldfish
don't like Jell-O!"

Activity 16

Oh, the Things We Have Learned!

Learning is a lifelong process—a series of miniscule and monumental adventures as people explore the world they inhabit. This activity, in which students interview people of all ages to find out what others have learned and are learning, brings this concept home to students in a way they find both interesting and enjoyable. By listening, sharing, and writing about both the big and small life lessons of others, students see that every day and every person in their lives is a potential source of knowledge or wisdom. They also recognize that life's lessons can be learned by people of all ages and that their own learning journeys will continue every day they live.

Learning Objectives

Through this activity, students will:
- think and work cooperatively on a class project,
- ask relevant questions and listen for information, and
- write about themselves and others within an assigned framework.

Materials

- Handout 16.1: What I've Learned
- Poster board or sturdy paper for making three signs

- Large index cards (one per student)
- Materials for making books (see Handout 3.1: Four Ways to Make a Book)
- Optional: *Oh, the Places You'll Go!* by Dr. Seuss and/or *Live and Learn and Pass It On* by H. Jackson Brown, Jr.
- For School Extensions and Variations: Poster board; pens, crayons, markers, or paints; construction paper; and ribbon or string

Time

One 45-minute session; additional at-home or inschool time to complete the activity and assemble the book

Preparation

Before beginning this activity, read Activity Step 2 and decide whether you wish to interview the three characters we suggest or three others whom you think will be familiar to your group of students and appropriate for their age levels. Create three signs labeled "Cinderella," "Abraham Lincoln," and "Harry Potter," or the names of other characters you've chosen.

Activity Steps

1. Gather together students and say: *Today we are going to meet some fascinating people who have a lot to teach us about ourselves and our world. In fact, these people are cleverly disguised, right now, as some of your classmates.*

2. Interview three characters. Invite a volunteer to the front of the class. Then, holding up the "Cinderella" sign for all to see, ask "Cinderella" questions about her life. For example: *What was it like living with your stepsisters? How did you first feel when you met the prince? How has your life changed since you've moved into the castle?* The last question to Cinderella should be: *After all of the experiences you've had, what have you learned about the goodness and badness of people?*

3. Ask similar questions of other student volunteers portraying Abraham Lincoln and Harry Potter, always ending with the same question: *After all of the experiences you've had, what have you learned about the goodness and badness of people?*

4. Point out to students that many of the things they learn in life come from interacting with the people around them. The things others say, the actions they take, and the advice they give all help students better understand the world. Explain that, with the help of parents, neighbors, and friends, students will compile a book of life lessons that incorporate some of these valuable nuggets of learning.

5. Share examples of life lessons. Display or distribute Handout 16.1: What I've Learned, which shows some life lessons compiled by children from our classrooms. Read aloud each of the life lessons about family, friends, school, self, and our world, asking for volunteers to interpret each statement. Then tell students that it is now their turn to compose some life lessons. You might also use examples from the book *Live and Learn and Pass It On*.

6. Brainstorm ideas in groups. Organize students into cooperative learning small groups and assign or let groups choose one of the categories listed on Handout 16.1. Tell students that they will brainstorm lessons they have learned about their group's category. Allow 5–10 minutes for brainstorming and then ask for students to read several of the statements they created.

7. Once the groups have finished sharing their life lessons, give every student an index card. Working individually, students should write three "I've learned" statements on one side of the index card, using any of the categories on Handout 16.1 or a new category that they would prefer.

8. For homework, students should ask family, friends, and neighbors to complete three or more "I've learned" statements on the back of the index card on which they wrote their own statements. They may choose one category or collect statements in a variety of categories.

9. Once the index cards have been completed and returned to school (we suggest no more than 2 days later), have students return to their cooperative learning original small groups. Distribute paper for the book pages and explain that group members should select from their combined lists and write 10–20 "I've learned" statements to be part of a class book. Emphasize that they should select statements that differ from one another as much as possible.

10. Optional: To make the point that students have learned a lot and still have many life lessons ahead of them, end the activity by reading *Oh, the Places You'll Go!* Or save this book for the "premiere unveiling" of the class book students have created.

For Surefire Success

Encourage students to ask for "I've learned" statements from people of varied ages and backgrounds.

School Extensions

- Have students illustrate the most humorous or meaningful life lessons on large, colorful posters. Hang the posters around the school.
- Compile a bulletin board of lessons learned by teachers, administrators, and school support staff. Place this in a highly visible place in the school.

Variations

- Use this activity as a project for the entire school and compile one large book to be placed in the office or media center for all to enjoy. Or have students trace their hands and write the lessons in the outlines. Display the hands by joining them with ribbon or string.
- Instead of a class book, have students write and illustrate their lessons on mini posters.

Handout 16.1
What I've Learned

Here are some of the life lessons learned by a group of students and their friends and families.

About Family

I've learned that parents can run more miles than kids.
—Age 7

I've learned that almost all 10-year-olds like to get paid for the things they do.—Age 64

About Friends

I've learned that a good pal doesn't care what kind of clothes you wear or how messy your hair is.—Age 11

I've learned that the most popular kids aren't always the best friends.—Age 12

I've learned that a couple of good friends are more important than a thousand casual friends.—Age 36

About School

I've learned not to play a big instrument and ride the bus.
—Age 10

I've learned that short kids sometimes get picked on.—Age 33

About Our World

I've learned that you shouldn't look up into the sun when
the teacher tells you not to.—Age 10

I've learned that I still have a lot to learn about the Earth.—Age 44

Activity 17

The Building Blocks of Character

All people have someone in their lives—or, if they are lucky, *many* some-ones—who has influenced them profoundly. In this activity, students select and write about this special person, acknowledging the gifts they have received from this individual. This is a great activity to use with other colleagues with whom you coteach during the year. The interactions that occur when teachers and students share their stories of the individuals who have affected their lives bring up honest emotions that everyone can share as a human family.

Learning Objectives

Through this activity, students will:
- recognize that people are interdependent,
- identify significant people in their lives,
- identify personal values,
- write their personal stories within an assigned framework, and
- give and accept constructive criticism.

Materials

- Handout 17.1: Two Building Blocks
- Handout 17.2: Building Block Template
- Pens, crayons, or markers
- Other decorative art materials
- Scissors

Time

One 30-minute session to introduce the activity; additional at-home or in-school time to complete it

Preparation

Arrange ahead of time for at least two colleagues (e.g., other teachers, the principal, support staff) to share with students their own stories about someone important in their lives. If these colleagues are willing to create and share their own "building block" instead of just relating the stories orally, that adds even more power to the depth of this activity. See Handout 17.1: Two Building Blocks for examples.

Activity Steps

1. Introduce the activity. In your own words, share the following sentiments with your students orally, or make up your own version of some pivotal moments in your students' lives:

    > Do you remember who taught you how to tie your shoes? Do you recall who taught you how to read or told you your favorite bedtime story? Can you think of a time when one of your friends or family members was available to listen and help when you were having a really bad day? Each of us has special people in our lives, people we will always remember, no matter how old we get. These significant people may be young or old, male or female; you may see them every day or only once a year. In other words, each of these important people in your life could be just about anyone.

2. Tell students they will be hearing from you and two other school adults about people who have influenced your lives. While you talk, students should take notes on the characteristics that made the people you and your colleagues talk about so important. Offer some examples of what qualities or actions made these individuals memorable: Were the people kind, helpful, funny, or patient?

3. Introduce the panel of adults (you and two coworkers) and share your stories. One by one, explain who the important person was/is that you have chosen and what makes the person so memorable. If you or your colleagues have chosen to design a "building block," now is the time to share those with students.

4. Speakers should keep the length to about 5–8 minutes. Be as specific and personal as your comfort level allows. When you are finished, allow students to ask you any questions they wish. Repeat this procedure for each panelist.

5. Have students work in small groups to discuss the specific characteristics they wrote down. Suggest that they also discuss how these characteristics enable people to affect the lives of others. Allow about 10 minutes for discussion.

6. Ask students to return to their individual places and think of an important person in their own lives who has some of the characteristics they were just discussing. Remind them that this could be a friend, relative, teacher, coach—anyone who has had a personal impact on them. Suggest that they jot down notes about who this person is and why the person has been so special in their lives. (*Note.* Depending on your time limitation, the next steps could take place immediately or on the following day.)

7. Once students have privately selected an individual who has helped to build their character, have them write a one- or two-paragraph description of why this person was important to them. As they finish, have them discuss the paragraphs with you and with one or two classmates for the purposes of editing. Students should revise their paragraphs, incorporating suggestions from you and their peers, to make their writing the best it can be. Emphasize that specific anecdotes or examples are much more effective than general comments like "My aunt was always there for me" or "He is a best friend I could talk to about anything."

8. Display or distribute Handout 17.1: Two Building Blocks and briefly discuss how the students wrote and illustrated the building blocks. Then, distribute 17.2: Building Block Template. Instruct students to carefully copy their paragraphs onto the blocks, reminding them to be sure their writing can be read easily. Encourage students to add some color and illustrations as well. Such additions really help the individual building blocks to stand out when they are posted on a wall.

9. When the building blocks are completed, post them in an array that resembles a wall, side by side, creating your classroom's or team's "Wall of Character."

For Surefire Success

- Be prepared for an emotion-charged adult panel. It's not often that teachers share with students some of their private thoughts about important people in their lives. Still, every time we have done this activity, we have found our students to be polite and respectful of our words and our emotions (spontaneous applause at the end of a panelist's comments is not uncommon). Also, because their teachers take this activity so seriously, students tend to do the same when it is their turn to think and write.

- You may find that many students will write about their parents. Some teachers initially see this as an "easy way out." We suggest you think twice before discouraging children from writing about their parents or caregivers. Many children deeply love and admire the adults with whom they live. Although some children do not live with one or both parents, these adults are still very important in children's lives. If they insist on focusing on two people instead of one (a mom and dad, perhaps), let them highlight both individuals.

Variation

If you do this activity with more than two classes, consider erecting several walls of character, each devoted to a different group of people: friends, grandparents, parents, siblings. Discuss ideas for these themes or categories with students.

Handout 17.1
Two Building Blocks

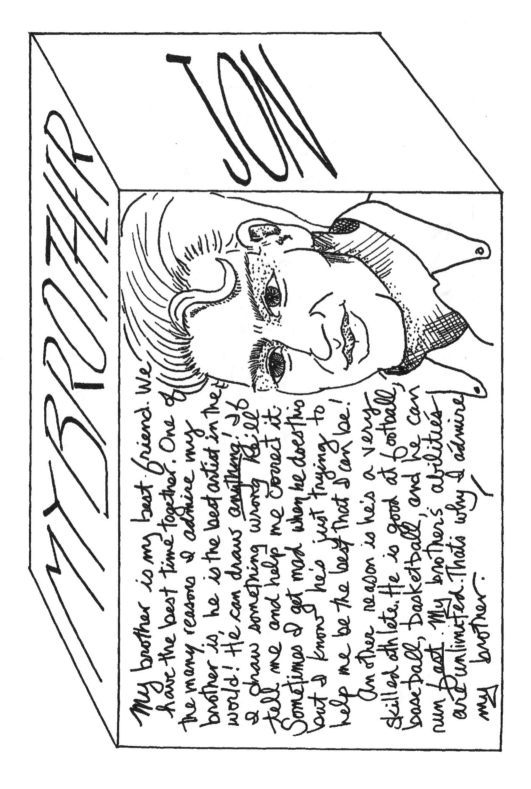

Handout 17.2
Building Block Template

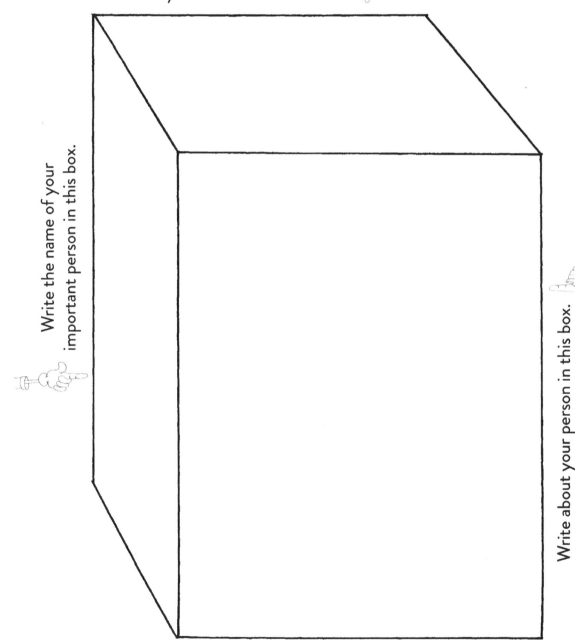

Write your own name in this box.

Write the name of your important person in this box.

Write about your person in this box. Add picture or decorations, too.

Activity 18

Shaking Hands With the World

The inspiration for this activity began with tragedy. Good friends of ours lost all of their possessions and their home to an inferno that engulfed their California residence. This was the second time in their lives that such a large-scale tragedy occurred, as one of these friends was a Holocaust survivor whose family had lost everything to the Nazis. At the time of this devastating fire, Jim was teaching fourth grade. He related this story to his students, who decided they wanted to help. How? Not by sending possessions to this couple, but by sending them messages of hope, goodwill, and strength. The kids called these messages "Helping Hands of Hope," and each was written on the outline of a student's handprint. Tying them together with ribbon, Jim sent these 29 pairs of hands (including his own) to a family member of this couple. Weeks later, the couple sent Jim's students their own set of handprints, with messages of love and gratitude.

Children care passionately about helping others, even people they don't know. Just as much, they care about their futures, as well as the health and well-being of the planet. This activity will help to bolster students' optimism and tap into their sensitivity by inviting them to offer messages of hope for the future of the world and to share those messages with others. By identifying their wishes for the future of the planet and their global neighbors, students begin to recognize the role each person can play as a steward of the Earth, an innovative problem solver, and a caring citizen.

Learning Objectives

Through this activity, students will:
- recognize that people are interdependent;
- identify personal values, beliefs, and interests;
- write their ideas within an assigned framework;
- demonstrate empathy for others; and
- refine their vocabulary.

Materials

- Handout 18.1: A Sampling of Hands
- Thesauruses
- Light-colored construction paper (one sheet per student)
- Scissors
- Single-hole paper punch
- Pencils and pens or fine line markers
- Colored pencils, crayons, or markers
- Other decorative art materials
- Ribbon or string for connecting hands
- Tape

Time

One 40-minute session; additional at-home and in-school time for decorating and connecting hands for display

Activity Steps

1. Display an image of a birthday cake with candles. Ask students for examples of specific times that they have wished for something. After a few ideas are offered, ask for specific examples of what students might wish for when blowing out the candles on a birthday cake. Write down their ideas on the board around the cake. Most students will identify material goods, such as new clothes or video games.

2. Next, change the scenario. Using characters well known to your students, such as Harry Potter, Minnie Mouse, Wonder Woman, or the Wizard of Oz, ask students what these characters might wish for as they blow out the candles on their birthday cakes. Provide a concrete example: "Harry Potter might wish for a new wand" or "Minnie Mouse might wish for a day off to enjoy the rides at Disney World." Expand the conversation by including other people, such as sports or TV stars, your city's mayor, students' parents, or the school superintendent. If you like, chart these wishes as well.

3. Share wishes and ideas for a peaceful, safer, or more beautiful world. Explain to students that they now must stretch their minds to think about the world and its inhabitants (people and animals) and about the future of the planet. Discuss how each person can wish for and contribute to world peace.

4. Tell students they will create a display called "Shaking Hands With the World." The display will include cutout hand tracings with students' ideas for improving their world, either on a grand scale (like curing a disease) or on a small one (helping people who have just suffered a personal loss in their lives).

5. Distribute and review Handout 18.1: A Sampling of Hands. Challenge students to think about wishes they might include on their own pair of hands. Explain that they should keep their ideas to themselves initially. Allow time for students to jot down some ideas that come to their minds.

6. The activity will proceed more smoothly if you help to facilitate students' thinking and writing. Assist individuals in expanding their ideas with different word selections. Encourage students to use a thesaurus for help with descriptive word choices instead of using more mundane terms like *happy*, *kind*, or *pretty*.

7. Have each student select a sheet of light-colored construction paper. Explain to them that they should use a pencil to trace their hands onto the paper, then carefully cut out the outlines of their hand shapes. Before students begin to write on the hands, have them punch two holes in their paper hands, one at the base of the pinky finger and one at the base of the thumb.

8. Ask students to write their wishes for the world or its inhabitants on their hand cutouts. Encourage them to use descriptive vocabulary in their writing. They may write on the hands in a variety of ways (e.g., one wish per finger or a poem on the palm). Once their writing is complete, have them decorate the hands with designs or small illustrations. Remind students to take care in decorating so their writing remains easy to read.

9. Weave the hands together using ribbon or string. The ribbon should go through one of the holes, behind the hand, and out through the other hole.

Allow 3–4 inches of ribbon between individual hands. A small piece of tape covering the ribbon on the back of each hand will help to keep the ribbon in place.

10. Hang the connected hands across walls in your classroom, in the hallway, or near the entrance of the school. You will find that a hallway display is very well received, even if it is created by a single class. Kids love to read the messages on the hands, which might also encourage other classes to join your parade of hands.

School Extension

Invite other classrooms, or even the whole school, to join your class in this activity.

Global Extension

This activity could easily be expanded to include other schools. Consider having a "hand exchange" with another classroom, either a local one or a classroom in a faraway place. Students might be surprised to read just how similar the wishes are for kids who live in very different parts of the country or world. The Teacher's Corner (https://www.theteacherscorner.net) is one of many resources that will help you find other classes wishing to connect on a project like this.

Handout 18.1
A Sampling of Hands

Here are some hands designed by fifth- and seventh-grade students:

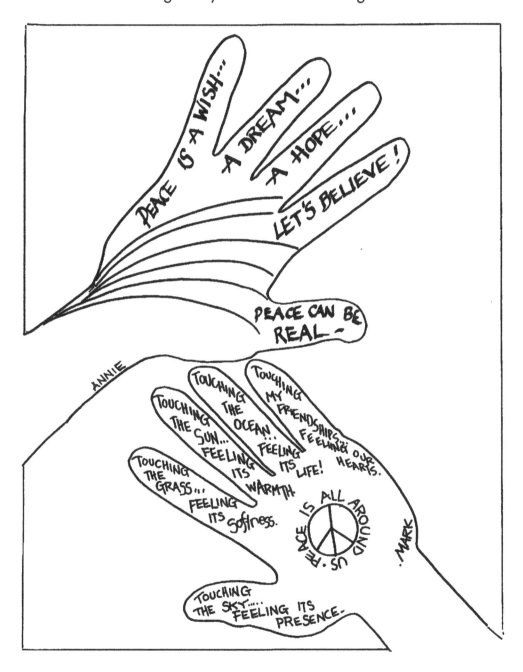

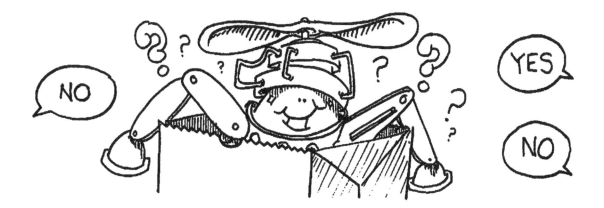

Activity 19

Guess It!

Curiosity is an essential ingredient of being human and developing healthy relationships. Through curiosity, people learn about the world and the people who inhabit it. This activity fosters students' curiosity while helping them refine and use their higher level thinking skills through questioning. Its implementation is easy; you simply choose both familiar and unfamiliar objects and invite students to guess what they might be. Your students' task, however, is more complex. Limited to asking "yes" or "no" questions, students are challenged to construct their questions in ways that will yield as much information as possible. In the process, students begin to understand the importance of using precise vocabulary to form concise and specific questions.

This activity takes little class time and can be done weekly or monthly. Introduce it early in the school year and keep students guessing each time as you introduce them to more and more objects about which they may or may not know much.

Learning Objectives

Through this activity, students will:
- think critically,
- ask questions to gain information,
- use vocabulary in a meaningful way,
- develop skills in using language,
- derive answers from context clues, and
- strengthen listening skills.

Materials

- Six coins
- One plain brown shopping bag with handles
- Various objects for students to guess
- Two or more sheets of chart paper or newsprint
- Marker
- Shoebox
- Strong brown paper for covering the box
- Scissors or sharp knife
- Packaging tape

Time

One 40-minute session to introduce the activity

Preparation

Decide how you will display the selected hidden objects so your students cannot touch or see them. For example, consider hanging the bag that holds the objects out of students' reach so they are not tempted to touch or squeeze it (yes, it's very tempting). Select the first week's object and place it in the "What Is It?" bag. Prepare a chart with two columns, one labeled "Yes" and the other labeled "No." (You may want to prepare additional charts for use in subsequent weeks.) Wrap the shoebox with brown paper and tape it securely shut. Cut a slit in the top of the box, which students will use to submit their guess. Put this box aside until needed.

Activity Steps

1. Tell students that you have six coins in your pocket or hands (jingle them so students can hear). It will be the students' job to figure out what coins you have and what their total value is by listening to the tone of the coins' sounds as they clink against each other and by forming essential questions requiring a "yes" or "no" response.
2. Have students work in groups of 3–4 to develop several questions that will help them determine the amount of money you have and the value

of each coin (i.e., how many dimes, nickels, etc.). Stipulate that you will answer only "yes" or "no" to any question. Stress that students should try to develop questions that will provide them with as much information as possible. Depending on the age of your students, you may want to challenge them to try to arrive at five questions to find the answer. (Some of our sixth graders accomplished this in four questions!)

3. Give an example of a question that yields little information (e.g., "Do you have 72 cents?"). However, "Are all of your coins silver?" is a better question, as it will eliminate pennies and help students take a step toward determining the coins' total value. Give students about 10 minutes to develop their questions before moving on to this next step.

4. After approximately 10 minutes, invite each group to pose their questions in round-robin fashion. Encourage students to listen carefully to others' questions and your responses as they may be able to ascertain the total

WHAT IS IT?   YES   NO

1. Is it something to eat?   ✓

2. Is it something one of us might play with?   ✓

3. Has Dino or Mark been playing with one like it before class?   ✓ (NO)

4.

5.

6.

7.

8.

9.

10.

value and the types of coins from others. If students "waste" questions—for example, by asking if there is a specific amount—stop them and remind them that their questions should be worded in ways that help gather as much information as possible. Try to enhance your students' listening skills by not repeating questions and answers, as it is very easy for students to get caught up in their own questions and continually yell out, "What did they ask? I didn't hear it!"

5. Once your students have asked their questions, ask each group to come up with a guess as to the correct amount of money and the value of each coin. Have each group explain the reasoning behind the solution. What clues did they get from the questions they asked that caused them to make the guesses that they did? You might want groups to write their responses down and hold up their papers simultaneously. If one or more groups guesses the correct amount of money, reward them with either a round of applause or something more tangible—a small treat or a "homework forgiveness pass," for example.

6. Explain the ongoing activity. Mention to your students that they will have an opportunity to continue to develop their questioning strategies. Every week (or month) you will display a "What Is It?" bag to tempt their curiosity and test their deductive reasoning skills. Inside you will place an object that may or may not be familiar to them. Students should guess the contents of the bag by posing a series of questions that can only be answered "yes" or "no." They may ask their questions before or after class.

7. Show students the "yes" and "no" chart (see Preparation) and explain that once you have answered a question, students should write that question in the appropriate column. You may choose to have a specific time each week for this activity, or you may prefer to take a few minutes each day during which students may ask questions about the object. If you choose the latter option, be sure to record the questions visually (e.g., on chart paper—complete with whether the answer to each query is "yes" or "no") so that questions do not get repeated during the week or month.

8. When a student wishes to make a guess as to the object's identity, they should write the answer and the date and time of the guess on a slip of paper, sign it, and place the paper in the shoebox that you have prepared.

9. At the end of the week or month, look through the papers in the box to see if anyone got the correct response. If more than one student guessed correctly, check the dates and times to see who guessed first. Ask those who guessed correctly to recollect which clues(s) were most helpful in determining the correct answer.

For Surefire Success

- Initially, you may have to include some questions of your own in order to spur students' thinking. Consider charting one or two questions the first couple of times you conduct this activity. For example, let's say you place a baby bottle in the bag. In a "yes" column, you may write "Would someone use this at home?" and in the "no" column, "Can this item be eaten?"

- Consider using objects that students may keep if they guess correctly, such as a small bag of candy. Or, include an object that may have been familiar to you but might be foreign to your students, such as a music cassette or landline telephone.

- Remind students that the general questions they asked that helped them identify the objects might also be useful in learning about new people they meet. So, instead of asking a specific question like "Are you in grade 5?", they might probe more deeply with a question such as "Do you have a favorite teacher or grade level so far?"

- Include a famous historical figure's photo or image in the bag and have students guess who this person is. This may be especially helpful in a specific content area (e.g., Marie Curie in science class). Too, you may wish to invite students to bring in their own unknown objects to be identified by classmates.

Activity 20

The Great Idiom Contest

Word puzzles: You've seen them and loved them. You've scratched your head only to see the obvious once the answers were revealed to you. Newspapers and magazines include them as a regular feature, and bookstores stock whole volumes devoted to them. What is it about word puzzles that sparks such interest?

This activity lets you pass on the fun of playing with language by challenging your students to create word puzzles for their classmates called "visual idioms." While creating their own visual idioms, students will explore countless other idioms that are part of the English language, which can be confusing to both adults and children alike—not to mention to English language learners. We have used this activity with a single class and as a friendly competition between two or more classes. Whomever you choose to include in this visual idiom activity, both fun and learning will result.

Learning Objectives

Through this activity, students will:
- analyze phrases and word usage,
- think and work cooperatively,
- communicate within an assigned framework,
- demonstrate creative and critical thinking skills, and
- expand their vocabulary and facility with language.

Materials

- Handout 20.1: A Sad (but True) Tale
- Access to Idiom Site (http://www.idiomsite.com) and/or the book *Hair of the Dog to Paint the Town Red* by Andrew Thompson

Time

Two 45-minute sessions

Preparation

Review the activity steps. Decide whether to conduct the activity within a single class or with two or more classes. Plan a way for each small group to work out of earshot of the others.

Activity Steps

1. Write or display some rebus word puzzles that represent idioms, such as these:
   - Head
     Heels
   - NUTinSHELL
   - HEA/RT

2. Ask your students to try to figure out what these odd word configurations mean. (These represent "head over heels," "in a nutshell," and "broken heart.") Then ask for volunteers to explain the meaning of each of these idioms. For example, is a "broken heart" really broken, or is this just an expression that conveys that someone is very sad?

3. Talk about idioms. Ask students: *Has anyone ever heard of the word* idiom? *Can you define what an idiom is?* Accept answers and discussion until you are sure all students understand the concept. An idiom is a phrase or expression that has its own unique meaning. The meaning goes beyond the individual words themselves—in fact, if you define the words one at a time, and then string the definitions together, the phrase doesn't make sense!

Each language has its own idioms, and idioms can't be effectively translated from one language into another.

4. Refer your students to http://www.idiomsite.com or *Hair of the Dog to Paint the Town Red*. Give some examples of idioms that they may find in either of these resources, such as:
    * the long and the short of it,
    * an open and shut case,
    * fit for a king,
    * on top of the world, and
    * a chip on your shoulder.

    Ask students what they believe each phrase means. Then ask if they can think of any ways to visually represent these phrases, *using only alphabet letters*—for example, the word "chip" on top of the word "shoulder" would be one way to represent the phrase "chip on your shoulder."

5. Next, distribute Handout 20.1: A Sad (but True) Tale and ask students to interpret the boxed words. (Wait to share the solutions to these boxed words until students have a chance to read through the story.) Within no time, you'll have students primed for the group activity, "The Great Idiom Contest."

6. Explain the contest. Tell students that there will be two large teams. Each team will break into small groups to brainstorm idioms and other phrases and create visual puzzles representing the phrases, similar to the ones found on Handout 20.1. Teams will then attempt to solve one another's word puzzles.

7. Divide students into two teams. Have each team's members break up into smaller work groups of three students. Give each small group an idiom dictionary or your prepared sheet of idioms. Have students write and draw as many visual idioms as they can within 20 minutes, using Handout 20.1 as a guide. Allow students to include some phrases, like "pigpigpig" ("three little pigs"), which is not technically an idiom, but can be displayed visually to add to the story's meaning. Each group should turn in to you its visual idioms and solutions.

8. Compile each team's visual idioms onto one page. If you feel creative, turn the puzzles into a story as shown on Handout 20.1. Compile solutions on a separate sheet.

9. Hold an idiom contest. The next day, or as soon as possible, place students in their original groups, challenging them to develop a story that uses as many of the visual idioms they have created collectively as possible. Remind them that the story they create must make sense, and not just be a random collection of visual idioms. Use an outside judge, such as the school

principal or another teacher, to determine which group created the most coherent and enjoyable story.

10. Divide teams into small groups of three, giving each group an idiom dictionary and a copy of the other team's visual word puzzles. Then, with the help of their logic and their dictionaries, students will have 20 minutes to try to decipher the other team's puzzles.

For Surefire Success

- Don't be too strict with your interpretation of idioms, at least not initially. Allow students time to get used to the idea that words and phrases can be expressed in numerous ways.
- A word of caution: If you use an adult idiom dictionary to share with your students, not all of the entries will be school appropriate. Most idiom dictionaries we've seen are unabridged. Safer bets for younger eyes are the two idiom resources we recommended for this lesson (see Materials).

Classroom Extensions

- As a creative follow-up to this lesson, have interested students turn their visual idioms and word pictures into a fairy tale, short story, or tall tale. Handout 20.1: A Sad (but True) Tale, created by a group of students and their teacher, made the rounds in our teachers' lounges and was included in a monthly parent newsletter—a good reminder that language can be as much fun as you want it to be.

- Display a visual idiom and ask for interpretations to begin the school day. These can be great icebreakers. There are plenty of online sources and books of idioms from which you may choose.

Handout 20.1
A Sad (but True) Tale

1. [ONCE / TIME] there were **2.** [PIG / PIG] who enjoyed **3.** [.¹DER] **4.** [gether / gether] .

One had a **5.** [L / eg] and the other a **6.** [Ar / ʾm] , but **7.** [AallLL]

they were as hoppy as **8.** [pppod] and as comfortable as

9. [R Bug BuqUG Buq] . **10.** [WHonceILE] the **11.** [Pig / pig] worried about things

Some silly **12.** [things / things] like the **13.** [BATH TUB] and some very

14. [THINGS / THINGS] like **15.** [WORpeaceLD] . They always **16.** [FiNGERS / FiNGERS] that

things would **17.** [TURN] O.K.

Now, **18.** [LISTEN] as I tell you a **19.** [TALE] that

will make your **20.** [HEAD HEAD HEAD HEAD] and give you a **21.** [Hear"t] .

I'll need your **22.** [ATTENTION X / ATTENTION + / ATTENTION −] .

Since the pigs were [23. BROKE] they needed some money. They hoped to earn [24. fi$$$st] in order to make [25. endsends], but their [26. WALL BACKS] because they were [27. School] [28. DROP] / [29. NUT in SHELL], the pigs couldn't even read. That's how they got into [30. TROUBLE]. They jumped into their car, a [31. BEAT] chevy. with [32. 4]. After they [33. Buckled], they took a [34. DRIVE] [35. COUN in TRY], hoping to find work that would help to put [36. food TABLE]. Instead, the pigs went [37. PAST] a sign that read [38. Construction ROAD]. They ended up going [39. head heels] over the [40. MOUNTAIN], hitting a [41. WATER!] on the [42. WAY]. It was so sad I almost [43. cried eyes] / [44. IT IT] is this: [45. SCH stay OOL] or else it's [46. Strike Strike Strike YOU'RE] in the ol' ball game. [47. THE]

Solutions:

1. Once upon a time
2. Two little pigs
3. Growing older
4. Together
5. Broken leg
6. Broken arm
7. All in all
8. Two peas in a pod
9. Three bugs in a rug
10. Once in a while
11. Two little pigs
12. Little things
13. Bathtub ring
14. Big things
15. Peace in the world
16. Crossed their fingers
17. Turn out
18. Listen up
19. Tall tale
20. Head spin
21. Broken heart
22. Undivided attention
23. Flat broke
24. Fistfuls of dollars
25. Ends meet
26. Backs were against the wall
27. High school
28. Dropouts
29. In a nutshell
30. Big trouble
31. Beat-up
32. Four on the floor
33. Buckled up
34. Long drive
35. In the country
36. Food on the table
37. Right past
38. Road under construction
39. Head over heels
40. Mountainside
41. Waterfall
42. Way down
43. Cried my eyes out
44. The long and the short of it
45. Stay in school
46. Three strikes, you're out
47. The end

Activity 21

Creative Inventors

This activity teaches creative problem-solving strategies with a touch of whimsy. Working cooperatively, students will invent a method or machine that solves a problem you present. Although humor will play a part in students' conceptions and designs, students will benefit from the larger lesson: People can collaborate for the benefit of others.

Learning Objectives

Through this activity, students will:
- work and think cooperatively and creatively,
- represent three-dimensional objects in a two-dimensional format,
- explain their ideas orally and in writing,
- recognize that there are many ways to accomplish a single goal, and
- reach consensus.

Materials

- Handout 21.1: Inventive Brainstorming
- Handout 21.2: Our Invention: How Will It Work?

- Unlined paper (one sheet per group)
- Chart paper or poster board (one sheet per group)
- Pens, pencils, colored pencils, or markers
- Large index cards (one per group)
- Optional: *The Wizard of Oz* by L. Frank Baum
- For Classroom Extension:
  - *Rube Goldberg's Simple Normal Humdrum School Day* by Jennifer George
  - *Build Your Own Chain Reaction Machines: How to Make Crazy Contraptions Using Everyday Stuff* by Paul Long
  - "World's Largest Rube Goldberg Machine Lights Up Christmas Tree" (https://www.youtube.com/watch?v=RBOqfLVCDv8)

Time

One or two 40-minute sessions; additional time for oral presentations

Activity Steps

1. Begin by reviewing with students the story of *The Wizard of Oz*. Ask students who know the story well to explain to those who don't know what this classic tale is about. If students don't mention that Dorothy returned to Kansas by wishing it so ("There's no place like home . . .") and snapping the heels of her slippers, mention this yourself. Focus on how Dorothy used her desire to return to Kansas—her home.

2. Divide students into groups of 2–3. Explain that each group has been hired by the Wizard of Oz to invent a creative new way to return Dorothy to her home in Kansas, just in case tapping her heels together doesn't work.

3. Distribute Handout 21.1: Inventive Brainstorming and ask the groups to generate, through brainstorming, a list of up to 20 possible ways to get Dorothy home. You might offer a couple of suggestions, both realistic and fantastical. A realistic idea would be to have the people of Oz hold a fundraiser to get Dorothy home by airplane, while a fantastical idea would be to locate one of the Wicked Witch's brooms and program it to land Dorothy back on her Kansas farm. Have each group select a recorder to list their ideas on the handout. When they have finished brainstorming, groups should mark the three ideas that represent their best, most creative thinking.

4. Allow each group to share their top three ideas with the class. Have the class reach a consensus about the best of the three ideas each group has

proposed. Although each individual group should be allowed to select their own best option, this classwide discussion of the options might be helpful in directing each group's final decision. Once each group has chosen its preferred option, distribute Handout 21.2: Our Invention: How Will It Work? Explain that students should discuss the ideas on the handout in preparation for drafting designs of their inventions.

5. Once each group's design decision has been made and discussed, have each group draft the design for their invention on a blank sheet of paper. Have students share their initial draft with you. Check to be sure they have included enough details so that others will recognize how their plan will work.

6. Once these rough drafts are finalized, have groups produce designs for their inventions on large, unlined sheets of chart paper or poster board. Students should work in pencil first, then use pens, markers, or colored pencils to complete their designs. Remind students to include a name for their group's invention on the final design.

7. Have each group draft and finalize a written explanation of how their invention works. Groups should write this explanation on an index card and attach the index card to their posters.

8. After all groups have completed their work, each group should present and explain its invention to the class.

For Surefire Success

- Monitor groups closely as they brainstorm ideas for their inventions. Encourage students to stretch their ideas by combining several of their original ideas into one.
- To help students get started, provide a "far-out" example, such as a giant rubber band used as a slingshot to shoot Dorothy back to Kansas.
- Prior to listening to the groups' presentations, you might want to think about some clever awards (e.g., Zaniest Idea, Most Expensive Idea) you can present to different groups for their completed masterpieces.

Classroom Extension

Introduce students to Rube Goldberg inventions, which present complicated solutions to very simple problems. Some good resources that might interest your creative, inventive students are listed on in the Materials section.

Handout 21.1
Inventive Brainstorming

Directions: You have been hired by the Wizard of Oz to invent a creative new way to return Dorothy to her home in Kansas. Start by brainstorming 20 ideas. When you've finished, select the three best ideas. Mark those three with an asterisk (*).

_____   _____
_____   _____
_____   _____
_____   _____
_____   _____
_____   _____
_____   _____
_____   _____
_____   _____
_____   _____

Handout 21.2
Our Invention: How Will It Work?

Directions: Before you design your invention, think and talk about how it will work. Use this sheet to help your thinking and planning.

1. What will we call our invention?

2. What will it do?

3. What materials will be used to make it?

4. How will it work?

5. What could go wrong? How can we prevent that?

6. How can we draw a plan for it?

Activity 22

Building a Book Report

Need an idea for a hands-on activity that brings reading to life? This project will entice most every student. First, students explore different reading genres and identify one they particularly enjoy. Next, they read and discuss their books with other students who are reading books in the same genre. As a culminating activity, students design and build a three-dimensional structure that represents their genre and displays their book reports.

This activity can be designed and carried out in a variety of ways, depending upon the age of your students, your curriculum needs, and your instructional style. The overall intent is for your students to become actively involved in "building" book reports. As they do, they'll also gain valuable experience in conceiving, planning, and carrying out a team project.

Learning Objectives

Through this activity, students will:
- think creatively,
- work and think cooperatively,
- plan and carry out a project over several weeks,
- symbolize both abstract and concrete ideas,
- represent three-dimensional objects in a two-dimensional format,
- plan and build three-dimensional structures,
- write within an assigned framework, and
- demonstrate effective decision-making skills.

Materials

- Handout 22.1: A Plan to Build Our Book Report
- Library books representing a variety of genres, such as mystery, science fiction, historical fiction, biography
- Chart or graph paper
- Markers
- Materials for building and decorating, such as poster board, cardboard, construction paper, rulers, tape measures, scissors, glue, and paints

Time

One 40-minute session to introduce the activity; additional in-school time to build models; one or two additional 40-minute sessions for sharing models

Preparation

Review the activity and decide how to help groups select genres. Be prepared to help students find different books in their assigned genres so that no title is read by more than one student.

Activity Steps

1. Discuss the term *genre* and the different genres of books. Help students identify their favorite genres by asking about the types of books they like to read. Use different library books to show examples of different genres. Tell students they will be exploring one genre by reading a book from that genre, talking and writing about it, and then building an object that represents the books they have selected.
2. Organize students into groups of 4–6. Explain that each group will choose and read books in one genre. Have a variety of books on hand from various genres, or conduct this activity in the media center or library for quicker access to more book titles. Titles should not be duplicated among groups.
3. Allow a reasonable amount of time for students to read the books they have selected. (We suggest a one-week minimum.)

4. Following the completion of the reading, have groups reconvene to discuss their books. After students have discussed their individual books, the groups should focus next on the genre itself and write their responses to these questions on chart paper:
   - What are characteristics of this genre?
   - What makes this genre interesting to readers?
   - How does this genre differ from books in other genres?

5. Explain that each group's next task is to select and build a three-dimensional object that will represent their designated genre. Discuss the meaning of "three-dimensional"; ask for examples (e.g., a dollhouse or LEGO structure). Make certain that students understand what it means to "represent" the genre. Offer some examples:
   - Students might design and build an eerie mansion to represent the genre of mystery. A summary of each of the books read by group members might appear in the windows of the house.
   - A group might create a 4-foot rocket to illustrate science fiction. Each rocket stage could represent one of the individual books read by group members.

   As noted in these two examples, part of the students' task will be to incorporate the summaries of their books into the object they construct. Depending upon the grade level of your students, you may need to offer some concrete ideas as to the types of structures they might build.
6. Have students discuss options and decide what to build. Encourage students to think creatively about how best to represent their genre.
7. After they have decided upon their desired object, students should draft a design on a sheet of chart or graph paper. Be sure they include a place for each of the summaries

of their books. Then have them list what materials they will need and who will be responsible for securing materials (other than those you are willing to supply). Distribute Handout 22.1: A Plan to Build Our Book Report. Give each group a set amount of time to complete construction, allowing for in-class time, as appropriate.

8. After students have completed their plans, the next challenge will be for them to construct the models.

9. Once all of the groups have completed their projects, take time for students to share their models and summaries with one another.

For Surefire Success

- Allowing class time to complete the projects will energize your groups. You can better encourage students to think creatively and to stretch their limits if this project is completed in school. Also, some students will have difficulty meeting each other outside of a school setting, so having them complete this project in school evens the playing field in terms of group cooperation and access to materials—and one another. It will also prevent the intervention of well-meaning adults who rush in to add more details and features (not that we have ever experienced such a situation . . .).

- Encourage students to help one another locate materials from home to complete their projects, such as an old dollhouse that can be transformed into a mystery mansion.

- If your school has a media specialist, team up with that person and tap into their expertise on various books students might choose to read.

- If your school has an instructional technology specialist on staff, you might consider the option of having some students build digital projects instead.

Classroom Extension

You can easily adapt this project to other content areas. For example, in social studies, students might build a structure to highlight their study of various peoples, events, or lifestyles: an Inuit snow house, a Navajo hogan, an Egyptian mummy case, a medieval castle, a Great Wall, a pyramid, or a covered wagon. The entire class can work together on one model and write brief, individual descriptions of the people, event, or lifestyle they have just studied.

Handout 22.1
A Plan to Build Our Book Report

Write a description of what you plan to build here: _____

_____

_____

_____

_____

What materials will you need? Where will you get them? List the materials here:

HANDOUT 22.1, continued

What tasks need to be done? Which comes first, second, and so on? When does each task need to be done? Write the tasks in order here:

1.		
2.		
3.		
4.		
5.		
6.		
7.		
8.		

Create a timeline for completing your project here:

Activity 23

Games to Go

Even with the omnipresence of video games today, most children are familiar with a variety of old-fashioned board games, such as Monopoly, Stratego, Chutes and Ladders, and others. This activity will help channel this interest and challenge your students with a truly comprehensive project: conceptualizing and creating their own board games. Throughout the several weeks they spend developing, testing, and refining their newly created games, students will stretch their skills in cooperation and problem solving to new limits. You will marvel at the level of originality many student groups are able to generate and sustain as they design their new board games.

Adapt the activity to fit any content area. This game-making project will breathe new life into any subject—geography, literature, biology, music, or mathematics—for both you and your students.

Learning Objectives

Through this activity, students will:
- learn the format of game boards,
- work and think cooperatively to design a board game,
- plan and carry out a project over several weeks,
- think spatially and utilize analytical reasoning,
- give and receive constructive criticism, and
- write directions within a standard format.

Materials

- Handout 23.1: Game Plan
- Handout 23.2: Playing the Game
- Several different board games, including some that are linear and have a short duration (e.g., Candyland) and those that are cyclical and take longer to complete (e.g., Monopoly)
- Chart paper or newsprint
- Adhesive tape
- Materials for making games (see What's in a Game? on p. 185)
- Videos:
  - "How to Make a Board Game" (https://www.youtube.com/watch?v=3QGSxy-72jg)
  - "Kids Board Game #2" (https://www.youtube.com/watch?v=SRiRw1RhHGA)

Time

Six to eight 40-minute sessions (most of this time is independent but monitored group work; some at-home or independent in-school time might be required in addition to class time)

Preparation

Determine the topic/subject of the game (e.g., science, fantasy, math facts) and any specific criteria students will need to meet before designing the game. For example, if the game will be related to the rain forest, decide what students will need to know about this topic before designing the game.

To ensure all students are familiar with some board games, you might want to have several available in the classroom and allow small groups to use class time to play and analyze the games.

To introduce your students to the basic elements of game design, show one or both of the videos mentioned in the "Materials" section of this activity. The information provided in these videos can be of great help to you and your students as they proceed with this activity.

What's in a Game?

Games can be constructed from the simplest to the most elaborate materials. Here is a good starter list:
- Pencils and erasers
- Rulers and yardsticks
- Tracing paper or carbon paper
- Scissors
- Scrap paper or cardboard
- Poster board or other larger display materials, or (if you are super adventurous) precut plywood
- Glue or rubber cement
- Ballpoint pens or fine line markers
- Permanent markers or paints
- Paper clips, straight pins, and pushpins
- Stencils or stick-on letters
- Construction paper
- Clear adhesive paper or laminating material
- Miscellaneous small objects, such as old game pieces, foam scraps, and bottle caps

Activity Steps

1. Ask students what their favorite board games are. List the games. Divide students into groups of 4–6 and select one of the listed games for each group. (*Note.* Students should be familiar with the board game they are assigned.) Ask group members to first focus on the board itself and to describe the pathway each player must follow (e.g., Do they move forward due to a roll of dice? Do they go around the board only once or multiple times before a winner is declared?).

2. Have students analyze the game's explicit directions. Be sure students understand that the directions for each game are written in a sequential, detailed format. Have groups share how their individual games should be played according to the game's rules. You may want to chart the group's explanations so that students can have a visual representation of the similarities and differences among the games.

3. Introduce students to the two basic formats of games: linear and cyclical. Linear games, like Candyland, involve moving a token from start to finish as quickly as possible. Cyclical games, like Monopoly, involve moving a token around and around one pattern and acquiring property or some other predetermined set of goods.

4. Challenge groups to develop a game of their own, listing the following steps, which are explained further in the next section of this activity. Explain that each group will:

   • Brainstorm game ideas.
   • Plan the type, design, and parts of the game.
   • Review and critique one another's plans as a way of troubleshooting and gathering additional ideas.
   • Create a mock-up and revise plans.
   • Construct the game and write directions.
   • Field-test the game.
   • Revise the game to improve it and correct problems discovered in field-testing.
   • Package the game.
   • Conduct the activity.

5. Proceed with the activity tasks listed in the next section.

6. Enjoy the games! Keep the games prominently displayed and available in the classroom. Remind students to treat the games carefully as they play and put them away.

Activity Tasks

Task A: Brainstorm. Encourage groups to start by thinking about the objective of their game. Explain that, in selecting the specific type of game they will make, each group must decide whether their ideas will best fit into a cyclical or linear format. For example, if the game will be based on a novel, the object might be to have a main character travel along a path of the story's settings and acquire items such as money, experiences, and clues (a cyclical format). Or, the game's tokens could represent main characters who need to get to a final destination as quickly as possible (a linear format). Remind students that they need to decide this first, before actually designing the game.

Task B: Plan the Game. The most difficult task begins after groups have chosen the type of game they will make. To facilitate this essential planning step, review Handout 23.1: Game Plan with students. Have each group tape a large sheet of chart paper to a table or the floor. This will serve as their planning map.

As group members brainstorm ideas, one student should record the ideas on the chart paper. After brainstorming, have the groups share their general ideas with the class. Encourage helpful comments and suggestions. (Sharing or revisiting the videos mentioned in the Materials section might be useful.)

Next, have students categorize their ideas into specific topics: rules, playing pieces, board design. Explain that once the ideas are categorized, it will be easier for students to discuss and determine which ideas will work best.

Task C: Review and Critique Plans. After each group reaches a consensus about the design of their game, have them work with another group to review their plans. It is essential to ask about the other groups game's objective (e.g., What will happen if a player lands on a "Challenge" square?).

Task D: Create Mock-ups. Using chart paper or cardboard, have each group make a mock-up of their game board. This is a critical step because students need to see a visual representation of their ideas. By looking carefully at the drafted design, students will be better able to evaluate if the decisions they've made, such as how a player advances, will actually work. They may decide to incorporate additional ideas, such as adding penalties or rewards for landing on specific spaces (e.g., "Move three steps forward" or "Lose a turn").

This mock-up also provides groups with a chance to revisit the original intent of the game. For example, if the game is supposed to be tied to a specific topic (e.g., rain forest protection), groups will need to decide if their plans include enough appropriate vocabulary and concept development to be meaningful to the game's theme. Counsel students, though, not to make their games too complex; otherwise they run the risk of losing the interest of their audience.

Task E: Construct the Game. Now it's down to the basics: actually constructing the gameboard and the playing pieces. Encourage students to work with a variety of materials. Suggest that poster board, construction paper, and plastic pieces or coins of various denomination for game tokens work well. Students will also need to consider the visual effect of their game. Is it attractive enough that other people will want to play it?

After assembling the game, each group will need to decide upon and write complete, precise directions. Remind students to proofread and edit all of their writing carefully. They'll want to check their spelling and grammar as well as the clarity of their step-by-step game-playing directions. Remind them that what seems clear to them might not be as clear to new players, so they must keep their instructions very specific. As groups write directions, stress the need for clarity and explicitness, referring back to published game instructions as necessary.

Task F: Field-Test the Game. Once the games are ready to be played, arrange a time for the groups to field-test them. You may elect to do this with the other groups that have worked on the project in your class or enlist students from other classes who are unfamiliar with the project. Have field-testers use Handout 23.2: Playing the Game to structure their evaluations.

Stress that field-testers should provide the game creators with helpful suggestions that will make the games more interesting or the directions easier to understand. Both you and the game-making groups should listen to how the field-testers explain the rules and progress around the board. Remind game designers not to interrupt the players with explanations. If the game needs to be explained, that is a clear indication that the design or instructions need to be fine-tuned.

Task G: Revise the Game. Have groups make changes based upon the field-testing. Meet with individual groups to discuss their progress.

Task H: Package the Game. Encourage groups to be creative in their packaging ideas. Have cardboard and other materials available for packaging. Remind students that it is best to recycle some materials; for example, students can turn an old laundry soap box into a game box or take a used trifold poster board and cover it with white paper to create a new game board. One potential extension is to have students develop a marketing plan for their new game (e.g., brochure, advertisement, etc.).

For Surefire Success

- This is a great activity for involving parent volunteers. As an individual teacher, it is often difficult to circulate among all of the groups and to provide as much help as might be required. Even one extra pair of helping hands from a parent volunteer is a welcome addition.
- Consider teaching a mini-lesson on the writing of directions. Simply use the directions from a published game to demonstrate how precise the game instructions are. Explain to students that, in writing directions, nothing should be assumed about the players' knowledge or understanding of how the game is played.

Classroom Extensions

- Have an interested student or group of students research how game publishers decide what makes a "good" game (i.e., the do's and don'ts of game construction).
- Have students research games of different cultures and create games based on the different formats they discover.

School Extension

Invite other classes to make games as well. Then, hold a schoolwide Games Fair featuring games and game playing. Include refreshments and prizes, and appoint a panel of judges to review the games. Invite families and others in the community to attend the event.

Community Extension

This activity lends itself well to a community project. Perhaps your students could design games for a local preschool or children's ward of a hospital.

Handout 23.1
Game Plan

Things to Consider

> Game type: Linear or cyclical?
> Object of game: To win the fastest? To collect the most coins?
> Rules: Step-by step instructions are a must!
> Playing pieces: How do they look, and what are they made of?
> Tricks
> Board design
> Scoring: How do you determine who wins?

Questions to Discuss

1. For what ages is the game intended?
2. Do players go around the board once or multiple times?
3. What might be the finishing point?
4. What is the object of the game?
5. How is the winner determined?
6. How many people can play (minimum and maximum)?
7. What is the suggested playing time?
8. What setbacks or obstacles might players encounter as they play the game?
9. How do players move forward?
10. If the game will have cards or a spinner, what will be on those items?
11. Will there be penalties or rewards for landing on certain spaces?

Handout 23.2
Playing the Game

Directions: As a game field-tester, you have a very important job. You need to let the game makers know what happens when you play the game. Use this sheet to write your comments.

1. Are the directions written clearly? If not, what do you not understand?

2. Does the game work like the directions say it will? If not, what didn't work?

3. How do you think the game makers could fix this problem?

4. Is the game too long, too short, or just right?

5. What do you like best about this game?

6. What other comments or ideas do you have for the game makers?

Recommended Resources

The following are descriptions and publishing information for the resources we recommend in the individual activities, plus a few more worth checking out.

Baum, L. F. (1982). *The wizard of Oz*. Holt, Rinehart, and Winston. (Original work published 1900)

> The original edition of this book was published in 1900 under the title *The Wonderful Wizard of Oz*. Many versions have been published over the years. The familiar movie adaptation is widely available.

Baylor, B. (1995). *I'm in charge of celebrations*. Aladdin.

> Imagine if there were a "Rainbow Celebration Day," a "Coyote Day," or a "New Year Celebration" that began on April 24. In this book, that's exactly what you get, as a young girl imagines all of the reasons to celebrate in her desert home. This book includes great ideas for creative and introspective thinking by students.

Brown, H. J., Jr. (1992). *Live and learn and pass it on: People ages 5 to 95 share what they've discovered about life, love, and other good stuff*. Rutledge Hill Press.

> A book of one-liners, this short volume details nuances about life that are well worth knowing. Examples include a 7-year-old who admits, "I've learned that you can't hide a piece of broccoli in a glass of milk," and an 80-year-old

who observes, "I've learned that a mule dressed in a tuxedo is still a mule." Fun and wisdom abound in this book.

Cooney, B. (1985). *Miss Rumphius*. Puffin Books.

Once, long ago, Miss Rumphius was a little girl named Alice who lived in a place by the sea. She had many dreams and goals, but her wise grandfather reminded her that she must do "something to make the world more beautiful." This award-winning picture book shows how Miss Rumphius goes about doing just that. In addition, several read-alouds of *Miss Rumphius* are available on YouTube.

Demuth, P. B. (2018). *What is the Constitution?* Penguin Workshop.

This book details the birth of the U.S. Constitution and how much the 55 signers of the document agreed and disagreed with what should be in it. The final result—a four-page document—has withstood the test of time for almost 250 years.

Denenberg, D., & Roscoe, L. (2016). *50 American heroes every kid should meet* (3rd ed.). Millbrook Press.

Recognizing that leaders come from all walks of life and all ethnic, racial, and economic groups, this book focuses on individuals who have made the world better with their leadership and passion. Historical and current figures include Rachel Carson, Thomas Edison, Sacagawea, John Glenn, Langston Hughes, Frederick Douglass, Roberto Clemente, Sandra Day O'Connor, Elie Wiesel, Yo Yo Ma, I. M. Pei, and others whose lives can inspire today's children.

The Editors of Conari Press. (2002). *Random acts of kindness*. Conari Press.

This bestselling book is a collection of short essays about people helping people for no reason other than shared humanity.

Games World of Puzzles. Kappa Publishing Group. https://gamesmagazine-online.com

With great ideas for creative and logical thinking, this bimonthly magazine offers dozens of intriguing puzzles and games guaranteed to stump even the most methodical thinkers.

George, J. (2017). *Rube Goldberg's simple normal humdrum school day*. Abrams.

Written by Rube Goldberg's granddaughter, this book follows school-age Rube, who sets out on a "typical" school day by overcomplicating every simple activity, from getting dressed to brushing his teeth. This great resource introduces students to the real-life Rube Goldberg in each of them.

Hoffman, M. (1991). *Amazing Grace*. Dial Books.

   This is the story of a young African American girl who wants to act the part of Peter Pan in her school play, even though people tell her she can't. This compelling story shares the power of positive thinking, self-confidence, and strong role models.

The Itch List. (2015). *John Goddard: The list and life of an adventurer* [Video]. YouTube. https://www.youtube.com/watch?v=92XYY-rCg8I

   This short video highlights the life of adventurer John Goddard who, at age 15, began compiling a list of things he wanted to do before he died, eventually committing to 227 items. One of his bigger goals was to kayak down the Nile River, which he was the first person to do. His book, *Kayaks Down the Nile*, details the adventures on the River that he and his two friends navigated successfully. Due to its age, the video itself is grainy, but the content is a powerful reminder of setting and keeping one's life goals.

Jones, C. F. (2016). *Mistakes that worked: The world's familiar inventions and how they came to be*. Delacorte Press.

   Coca-Cola, sticky notes, Frisbees, cheese, chocolate chip cookies, and aspirin—all are inventions that happened by accident. This delightful book gives new meaning to the word *oops* as it explores the beauty of not being perfect and of using creativity to make the best of a bad situation.

Kohn, A. (2018). *Punished by rewards: The trouble with gold stars, incentive plans, A's, praise, and other bribes* (25th anniversary ed.). Houghton Mifflin Harcourt.

   Put away your stickers and your desktop marble jars! According to Kohn, rewards like stickers and marbles send the wrong message to students as they take away the intrinsic desire to learn and replace it with empty external rewards—controversial, to be sure, but worth a good, long read.

Long, P. (2018). *Build your own chain-reaction machines: How to make crazy contraptions using everyday stuff*. Quarto Books.

   The title says it all: The author creates 13 zany and complicated mechanical contraptions using ordinary stuff you'd find around your house. A mechanical engineer, Long gives step-by-step instructions for making low-tech devices that flip a light switch, squeeze toothpaste, make music and more. This resource is great for kids interested in STEM or learning to be more creative.

Ludwig, T. (2013). *The invisible boy*. Knopf Books.

   This picture book for children up to grade 5 introduces Brian, a boy who is never asked to birthday parties or to join in groups at school, and, in general, leads a lonely and solitary life. When a new boy, Justin, joins Brian's class, Brian befriends him—to the advantage of everyone involved. This book shows how small acts of kindness (and *unkindness*) affect people.

Manes, S. (2018). *Be a perfect person in just three days!* Cadwallader & Stern.

Caught up with the urge to be perfect in social and academic ways, a young boy learns the beauty of making mistakes from a wise and wacky professor. This is a great read-aloud book (and is also available as a video).

Mora, P., & Martinez, L. (2016). *I pledge allegiance.* Dragonfly Books.

Libby's great aunt, Lobo, lives in the U.S. but was born in Mexico. She needs to recite the Pledge of Allegiance as a part of her U.S. citizenship qualification. Libby is also learning the Pledge in school, so Lobo and Libby practice together and, in doing so, share stories and memories from their lives.

Pasricha, N. (2010). *The book of awesome.* Putnam.

After several unsettling life events, Pasricha decided to amass as many positive small things as he could to make himself feel better. His blog, 1000 Awesome Things (https://1000awesomethings.com), won an award for its inventiveness and led to his *New York Times* bestselling book in which he highlights small things to celebrate, like "things you were going to buy anyway being on sale," "the smell of crayons," and "fixing electronics by smacking them." This is a joyous ride through life's smallest pleasures.

Piper, W. (1976). *The little engine that could.* Platt & Monk.

A train filled with toys cannot ascend a hill to get its presents to the children who are looking forward to receiving them. Several larger locomotives refuse to help, but a small blue train whose mantra is "I think I can . . . I think I can" helps the train move forward and get its presents to the thankful children. This classic children's book has been a favorite for generations—with good reason, as it shows the power of perseverance and positive thinking.

Seuss, D. (1961). *The sneetches and other stories.* Random House.

When an entrepreneur moves into town with a machine that puts stars on residents' bellies, everyone wants one—but they can't all have one. What results is a classic no-win situation where competition and greed win out over common sense and cooperation. This marvelous story is perfect for young and old alike.

Seuss, D. (1988). *Oh, the places you'll go!* Random House. (Original work published 1960)

> A fitting gift to give at graduation or transition points in anyone's life, this creative, thoughtful book will make readers appreciate the beauty and fear that accompany change.

Smith, M. G. (2016). *My heart fills with happiness.* Orca Book Publishers.

> The sun on your face, the smell of bread baking, holding the hand of someone you love—all small things worth celebrating! This book for young children explores the many things people take for granted that enrich their lives, giving these small things the importance they deserve.

Sundem, G. (2010). *Real kids, real stories, real change: Courageous actions around the world.* Free Spirit.

> Biographies do not have to be about famous dead people. This book gives students a chance to see that everyday heroes exist all around them, even in their very own school.

Terban, M. (2007). *Mad as a wet hen!: And other funny idioms.* Clarion Books.

> In this book, students learn both the meanings of idioms and how they came to be a part of our language and culture. A great resource for showing kids that reading, writing, and speaking can be fun!

Thaler, M. (2008). *The teacher from the black lagoon.* Scholastic. (Original work published 1989)

> What happens on the first day of school when the teacher, Mrs. Green, turns out to be a real dragon? This is a hilarious story about beginning-of-the-school-year fears.

Thompson, A. (2017). *Hair of the dog to paint the town red: The curious origins of everyday sayings and fun phrases.* Ulysses Press.

> This compendium of dozens of common idioms and their underlying origins will entice students who love the fun and complexity of language. It's 99% okay to use with students, with only one or two idioms that might not be appropriate in class.

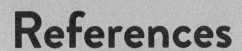

References

Jones, C. F. (2016). *Mistakes the worked: The world's familiar inventions and how they came to be*. Delacorte Press.

Pocock, J. (2017). *Are we spoiling our kids with too much praise?* JSTOR Daily. https://daily.jstor.org/are-we-spoiling-our-kids-with-too-much-praise

Purkey, W. W., & Novak, J. M. (1996). *Inviting school success: A self-concept approach to teaching, learning, and democratic practice* (3rd ed.). Cengage Learning.

About the Authors

Deborah S. Delisle is the president and CEO of the Alliance for Excellent Education (All4Ed), a Washington, DC–based national policy, practice, and advocacy organization dedicated to ensuring that all students, particularly those who are traditionally underserved, graduate from high school well prepared for success in college, work, and citizenship. Previously, Deb served as executive director and CEO of ASCD, a professional community of more than 120,000 education professionals around the world. She was nominated by former President Barack Obama, and approved by the U.S. Senate, to serve as U.S. Assistant Secretary of Elementary and Secondary Education from 2012 to 2015.

Deb has extensive experience at the local, state, and national levels. She served as Ohio's 35th state superintendent of public instruction and was the superintendent of the Cleveland Heights–University Heights City School District. Deb has served on several education-related boards and received numerous honors, including having a school named after her in honor of her lifetime of service to students. In July 2014, she was identified by the *National Journal* as one of five women in America who influence and shape national education policy.

James R. Delisle, Ph.D., has worked with and for gifted children and teens for more than 40 years. The author of 25 books and hundreds of articles, Jim's career has focused on understanding the social and emotional needs of gifted individuals, as well as integrating social and emotional learning into language arts instruction. A retired Distinguished Professor of Education at Kent State University, Jim continues to work with gifted teenagers on a monthly basis, a commitment he has made for the past 2 decades.